HADDON
THE
HEAD HUNTER

A. C. HADDON, 1924

*From the painting by P. de László now in the
Museum of Archaeology and Ethnology, Cambridge*

HADDON

THE HEAD HUNTER

A SHORT SKETCH OF THE LIFE OF

A. C. HADDON

by

A. HINGSTON QUIGGIN

CAMBRIDGE

AT THE UNIVERSITY PRESS

1942

CAMBRIDGE UNIVERSITY PRESS
Cambridge, New York, Melbourne, Madrid, Cape Town, Singapore,
São Paulo, Delhi, Dubai, Tokyo, Mexico City

Cambridge University Press
The Edinburgh Building, Cambridge CB2 8RU, UK

Published in the United States of America by
Cambridge University Press, New York

www.cambridge.org
Information on this title: www.cambridge.org/9780521166324

First published 1942
First paperback edition 2010

A catalogue record for this publication is available from the British Library

ISBN 978-0-521-16632-4 Paperback

CONTENTS

ILLUSTRATIONS

vii

PREFACE

THE life history of Alfred Cort Haddon is, to a great extent, the life history of modern Anthropology, concerned with the rescue of 'the Cinderella of the sciences' from the dusty—even smutty—hearth, and her introduction into the august society, if not of Princes, at least of Universities and University dons. The stages in the growth of Anthropology have been described thus:

> First a heap of heterogeneous facts and fancies, the leavings of the historian, of the adventurer, of the missionary—the favourite playground of *dilettanti* of various degrees of seriousness; next we see order arising out of chaos and the building up of a number of superstructures, bearing the signs of transitoriness and imperfection; finally to be replaced by the solid fabric of a coherent whole.

> *History of Anthropology*, 1910, p. 1.

The man who contributed most to making the foundations of the solid fabric sure and raising the subject to the status of an exact science based on observed fact was A. C. Haddon. Throughout his life he had little encouragement and little material reward. His brief periods of schooling ended with entry into his father's office when he was fifteen, so his self-taught science had to be squeezed into odd hours of leisure, but he had a passionate desire to learn all about everything and to see things for himself. Cambridge in 1875 opened the doors of a new world in which he soon made his mark, and after brilliant work in his Tripos, and later as Demonstrator he was

appointed Professor of Zoology in Dublin in 1880. His
visit to Torres Straits in 1888 was the turning point in
his career. He went out as a marine biologist. He
returned to devote the rest of his life to the study of
Man. In 1893 when he settled in Cambridge Anthropology still had dubious associates, but within thirty
years, during which Haddon was virtually its only ex-
ponent in the University, it was raised to its present
honoured position, with a flourishing school sending out
its students to all quarters of the globe. In his *History
of Anthropology* Haddon honours the names of the
pioneers. This sketch attempts to describe and com-
memorate one whose name is worthy to be placed with
theirs, whose work it was, if not to create the science of
Anthropology, to mould Anthropology into a science.

ACKNOWLEDGMENTS

Thanks are due to many friends and correspondents,
especially to Mrs Holland Rose and Mrs Rishbeth for
help with the earlier and later chapters; to Dr Praeger,
Mr F. M. Steele and Mrs Thompson for details of the
Dublin period; and to Miss G. L. Elles, Miss L.
Whitehouse and Miss O'Reilly for items of information
and for criticism of MS. or proofs.

A. H. Q.

March 1942

CHRONOLOGICAL TABLE

1855   Born May 24.

1866   City of London School.

1867–8 Mill Hill School.

1870   Printing Office, Bouverie Street, London.

1875   Christ's College, Cambridge.

1879   B.A. degree. Zoological Table at Naples. Appointed
        Curator of Zoological Museum, and Demonstrator
        in Comparative Anatomy, Cambridge.

1880   Appointed Professor of Zoology, Dublin.

1881   Married Fanny Rose.

1887   *Introduction to the Study of Embryology.*

1888–9 Expedition to Torres Straits and New Guinea.

1893   Home in Cambridge.

1894   *Decorative Art of British New Guinea.*

1895   Appointed Lecturer in Physical Anthropology, Cam-
        bridge.
        Evolution in Art.

1897   Sc.D. degree, Cambridge.

1898   *Study of Man.*

1898–9 Cambridge Anthropological Expedition to Torres
        Straits.

1899   Elected F.R.S.

1900   Appointed Lecturer in Ethnology, Cambridge.

1901   Elected Fellow of Christ's.   Dublin Professorship
        resigned.
        Head-Hunters. Reports, vol. II, i.

1903   *Reports*, vol. II, ii.

1904   Board of Anthropological Studies established, Cam-
        bridge.
        Reports, vol. v.
        Martin White Lectureship, London.

1906	*Magic and Fetishism.*
1907	*Reports*, vol. III.
1909	Appointed Reader in Ethnology, Cambridge.
	Races of Man.
1910	*History of Anthropology.*
1911	*Wanderings of Peoples.*
1912	*Reports*, vol. IV.
1914	Percy Sladen Trust Expedition to Papua.
1917	Y.M.C.A. France.
1920–2	Acting Curator of the Museum of Archaeology and Ethnology, Cambridge.
	Man, Past and Present (ed.).
1925	70th birthday. Resigned Readership.
1931	Golden wedding.
1935	80th birthday.
	Reports, vol. I.
	We Europeans.
1936	*Iban or Sea Dayak Fabrics.*
1936–8	*Canoes of Oceania.*
1940	*Smoking and Tobacco Pipes in New Guinea.* (In the Press.)
	Death. April 20.

Chapter I

CHILDHOOD AND BOYHOOD

1855–1875

———————

ALFRED CORT HADDON was born on May 24, 1855, the first son and second child of John Haddon, Printer, of London, and of Caroline (née Waterman) his wife.

But that is not how a biography should begin. The life of a man and the work that he did cannot be comprehended within the bounds of his own span of years, even though they number four score and five; destiny has been busy for generations, and the foundations are laid in the lives and characters of his forbears and the influences of his home.

It is curious that anyone so convinced of the importance of heredity as was A.C.H. should have been so reticent and indeed careless about his own. He openly despised that form of ancestor worship that engenders or is engendered by snobbery, and was far more deeply interested in the genealogies of the Torres Straits Islanders than in that of the Haddons; he maintained a life-long devotion to his younger sister and a keen interest in all his relatives, but he was far too much occupied in planning the family future to bother about its past.

Fortunately the family tree has been preserved in 'the stud book' as he called it, which contains a diligent account of 'the numerous Haddons who in many walks of life have done their duty in bygone centuries and contributed no unworthy share to the building up of the national life of England'.[1] The book contains reproductions of the portraits of many of the Haddon worthies and these are significant.

There is the great-grandfather John (1744–1818), a pleasant-looking curly-haired gentleman-farmer of Naseby, farming the land, still open field, over which the famous battle was fought a century earlier, and ploughing up the bullets which his sons collected as treasures. He joined the Baptists when to do so attracted contempt and derision which developed into open hostility; but opposition only stiffened his convictions. His house was licensed for preaching and he had many preachers and missionaries among his guests, for he was especially interested in foreign missions, to which he gave practical support, financing the training of his own farm bailiff to become a missionary in India.

The portrait of his son, also John Haddon (1784–1855), shows that he was not destined for a farmer's life. He has the face of a scholar and was noted for his literary tastes, though it was as a business man that he made his mark. He was apprenticed to a printer at the age of fifteen, and after a year went to London to seek his fortune. In 1814 he founded the printing business which celebrated its centenary in 1914 with a booklet 'set in Haddon types and printed throughout on up-to-date machinery supplied by John Haddon & Co.' This John, like his father the farmer, was a strong Nonconformist, but not a narrow-minded one. 'I prefer to find points of

W. G. Cruft, *A History of the Haddons of Naseby*. 1915.

contact, not of difference, with my fellow Christians', he used to say, and he showed his indifference to the socio-religious conventions of his day by himself escorting his youngest sister to Gretna Green to be married to her sister's widower. He was closely associated with the Baptists and printed much of their literature, especially that for foreign missions, in which, like his father, he was particularly interested. The missionaries, many of whom were personal friends, used to ask for goods to be sent out with the books and pamphlets, and so the general commission agency grew up which brought John Haddon and Co. in touch with all parts of the world. John Haddon's second wife was a Miss Cort from whom her famous grandson took his second name. She had been given the best education to be had in her day, and evidently profited by it, for she was a highly cultured woman, handing on her love of poetry and her skill as an artist (Bonington, Turner's master, was her teacher) to her eleven children. Their home is described as being

ruled by single-minded Christian folk, caring intensely for all movements making for righteousness and the good of the people; with limited means and eleven children; entertaining very constantly all sorts of philanthropists and missionaries, and using hospitality unstintingly to all who needed it.... A good education for all was reckoned a necessity, and interest in religious and philanthropic causes a serious duty.[1]

The eldest of these eleven children was the third John Haddon (1823–1904), who after his apprenticeship entered his father's business and became sole proprietor in

[1] H. M. B., *Five Sisters and a School*. 1905.

1855. But philanthropy and religion interspersed with music and gardening were nearer his heart than business and the business suffered in consequence. He trustfully entered into unsuccessful partnerships and the family fortunes are reflected in the constant moving from house to house and the difficulties in meeting the increasing expenses of the growing family. In the 60's his children's early recollections were of country houses outside London, of large gardens and of neighbouring woods in which they ran wild. In the 70's and 80's these spacious memories are replaced by fainter impressions of a succession of houses in New Barnet, in Finchley, in Lewisham and in St George's Road, Wimbledon. Their mother recognises as among the crosses she has to bear that she must appear stingy in housekeeping, having 'to put on the screw and seem grudging over little things, being under-servanted and considered a bad manager....But I say to myself "*He* knows, even if my husband doesn't".' In 1888 a cousin, Walter Haddon, joined the firm as a partner and he became sole proprietor in 1890. Thenceforward the business prospered and grew into the world-wide position which it occupies to-day. But John Haddon's active interest in it came to an end.

The portrait of this John Haddon, the Baptist deacon and constant Sunday school teacher up to the age of seventy (Pl. I), has been likened to that of the Deity in *Green Pastures*, and it suggests that there may have been some lack of common sympathy between him and his original and irreverent son. But there was no divergence of views and no irreverence throughout the period with which this chapter deals.

PLATE I

JOHN HADDON

MRS JOHN HADDON

A.C.H. as schoolboy

A.C.H. as undergraduate

The picture of John's wife and Alfred's mother (Pl. I) is a happier and a livelier one. She used to quote

> Round how mere a log did twine
> Those frail tendrils of the vine,

the log representing her revered but unimaginative husband, round whom she dutifully and affectionately twined for forty-five years. Caroline Waterman was twenty-six when she married John Haddon, at Highbury Chapel, Bristol, on March 29, 1853. With characteristic juxtaposition of business, sentiment and a somewhat ponderous attempt at humour the bridegroom writes on March 31:

I should like to pay off the £100. Can you call here or meet me in the City any hour? John is no longer his own Master—he now lives to please his Lady. Last Tuesday was the happy day at Bristol. P.S. You will have cards.

Their first child, Edith, was born before the year was out; Alfred came seventeen months later (May 24, 1855); Laura in June of the following year. So there were three children under three to look after. Mrs Haddon turned her full-time job to good account. She devoted herself to her children from the first, and as they grew older, taught them their lessons and took them for walks, spending long picknicky days in Hadley Woods close by, giving that best form of education, sympathetic and intelligent companionship. But all the time she was writing. She wrote numerous anonymous articles for various periodicals, all on religious topics, and she published several books under the name of Caroline Hadley. Necessity is the mother of much literary effort, and the first necessity was to add to the dwindling family income to meet the increasing family expenses. So the walks with the children and their daily education became her sources of inspiration. The stories she told them—all out of the Bible—were published as *Stories of Old, Stories of the New Testament* and *Stories of the Apostles*; *Children's Sayings* (1862) shows the reactions to her teaching. Best of all, *Woodside, Look, Listen and Learn* (not published until 1887) shows the training of the children in what we should now call Nature Study. This book was a great success and ran into a second edition. But the greater success came in 1901, when A.C.H. dedicated his *Head-Hunters* 'to my Mother who first taught me to observe'.

Children's Sayings is a set of moral tales based on familiar outbursts such as 'I can't do it' (Alfred); 'I will, I won't' (Edith); 'It doesn't matter' (? Laura). Alfred has a chapter all to himself with a story of a spelling lesson, which ends with

Alfred was of a very loving nature and he found that if he really wanted to help others he must take a great deal of pains and trouble himself. So love made him painstaking and painstaking did not bring trouble but happiness.

No amount of painstaking ever made him an impeccable speller, and when he came to write books for himself he always kept a dictionary within reach and never allowed a doubtful word to pass unconfirmed. Probably the memory of what he learnt at his mother's knee was enshrined in his favourite quotation from John Ray, 'Nothing is insuperable to Pains and Patience'.

Whether from choice or from necessity Mrs Haddon undertook the education of the children from their early

years, and her sister, 'Aunt Agitate' as they disrespect-
fully called her, took over the work when Mrs Haddon
was preoccupied with the new baby, Arthur Trevor, who
was born in 1864.

This was a time of happy healthy childhood. Edith,
whose nickname was 'Peacock', always a little aloof;
Alfred and Laura ('Spitfire') always in and out of scrapes
and always together. They were allowed to do much as
they liked, and, in overalls, to get as dirty as they liked,
an unusual privilege in those days. They collected everything, from little bits of quartz or coloured stones in
rubbish heaps to precious rarities and curiosities from
overseas; they ground down pieces of brick to make
coloured paste; they collected the usual caterpillars,
moths, butterflies and birds' eggs and kept a slowworm
in the house until it disappeared as is the way with slow-
worms. The sisters helped their brother, who was the
collector-in-chief, and his special treasures were preserved in bottles. All the second-hand shops within
reach were ransacked for bargains, though the diaries
record whole afternoons spent going from shop to shop
without making a purchase. Even in these early days he
earned the title of 'head-hunter' which clung to him
through life, for somehow or other he acquired some
human skulls. He hoped to scare his sisters with them,
placing them, dimly illuminated, in a row on a shelf,
turning out the light and hiding the matches. He was
disappointed when the girls showed no alarm.

There was one great advantage derived from the
father's business, however much detested in later days;
paper, pencils and pens were abundantly supplied and

constantly in use. John Haddon was himself a good black and white artist and took his sketch-book with him wherever he went. His son used to say—and to prove—that 'a poor sketch is worth a page of description', and some of his early sketches are preserved in a scrap-book. There is 'My First Horse (the first drawing I remember doing. 1864. aged 9)', whose anatomical impossibilities are drawn from memory, not from observation. A livelier elephant follows in 1866, and on the same page comes the picture so familiar later as a slide in his lectures on Art or Ethnography, of the Bushman hunter disguised as an ostrich. The subjects are mostly animals and copied from books, but there are sketches from nature made on an exciting visit to Minehead when the train broke down on the branch railway as he records in his note-book. The adventure is described and illustrated by a sketch of the uncoupled train. There are also sketches of the quay, the church, with an ambitious attempt at the complicated interior, and the bathing beach 'with the only two machines'; similar but better finished sketches in John Haddon's book show that father and son were working side by side.

The collection of sketches reflects the boy's tastes and soon shows increasing skill in drawing birds and butterflies (from books) and silkworms (his own); later come a 'fancy geological composition' full of prehistoric beasts, and (after he had obtained the feather of a wild peacock from obliging Uncle Ferguson in Ceylon) 'Sketches illustrating Darwin's theory as to the development of the ocelli of the Peacock from actual specimens. 1871'. These are finely drawn with infinite care and patience. This habit of making sketches correct down to the minutest detail to illustrate his notes was invaluable for his later work. Accuracy rather than artistic production was the one thing aimed at; he drew, as he wrote, not to please the eye, or the ear, but faithfully to register facts.

His schooling seems to have been scrappy and precarious. For some time after the tutelage of 'Aunt Agitate' he went to a dames' school for small boys and girls at Highgate, kept by the Misses Gostell. Miss Gostell was a pioneer in her day, and he owed much to her teaching as he gratefully acknowledged. Many years afterwards she was still lending him books on geology 'to keep as long as you like', and he gave practical proof of genuine friendship by consenting to act as groomsman when the younger Miss Gostell was being married.

For a term or two in 1866 he was at the City of London School,[1] and from January 1867, when he was eleven, to June 1868, when he was just thirteen, he was a boarder at Mill Hill, then well outside London. This school, which had been founded with such high hopes and high principles early in the century to provide education for the sons of dissenters (ineligible for entrance at the established schools), was then at its lowest ebb, and the numbers had dropped from the hundred for whom it was designed to thirty or forty. The fees (fifty-three guineas a year inclusive) allowed scarcely enough for board and lodging and no margin for upkeep. The assistant masters (at £60 to £80 a year) were mostly transient and ineffective. Headmasters in quick succession attempted

[1] Cf. A. E. Douglas-Smith, *The City of London School*, 1937, p. 159.

to restore prosperity but in vain, and the school was closed down in December 1868.

A.C.H. was at Mill Hill for some eighteen months when the school was at its worst, so although he maintained an interest in it, and was gratified at being asked to preside at the Old Millhillian Club in later years, it never held a high place in his affections and he left without regret. For the next few years he went to any school which happened to be in the neighbourhood as the family moved from suburb to suburb, supplementing such scrappy education by evening classes. He was destined for the parental business of printing and spent a year in a drawing office, doing various odd jobs for his father meanwhile. He designed *carte de visite* mounts (which he despised as 'very silly concerns'),[1] show cards and note-paper headings, and developed that keen eye for patterns, which is detected in his writings on Art. He spent much time on cards and valentines on his own account, and in copying out notes and illustrations from borrowed books on natural science and travels. But his main interests were in his collections of plants and animals, live or bottled, in his insectarium or his aquarium, in dissections and micro-scope work.

Diaries from 1872 (1873 is missing) to 1875 when he came up to Cambridge give some idea of his home life, the large (mainly Nonconformist) circle in which he grew up, his deep religious convictions, his wide interests, his physical energy and his entire devotion to natural science, whether botany, geology or zoology, especially the latter,

---

[1] He was much gratified when his father gave him 9s. for these, and he bought a pocket lens with the money (March 26, 1872).

10

almost all self-taught by reading and observation.[1] The inconsequences and arbitrary juxtapositions of the entries in a pocket diary give it a special charm, particularly when the topics are so varied and every important detail has to be noted. It is difficult to believe that the youth whose crowded diaries contain no illegible word, who kept such careful records, who rarely mentions even a game without noting the winner and the scores, or a party without a list of the guests, could be so careless that he was considered worse than useless in the office. But the diaries help to explain.

In August 1874, his father was not well and was advised to take a long holiday, so he turned over his responsibilities to his son and went with the rest of the family to Cornwall for a month. This was a busy time. Besides the office duties there were all the usual prayer meetings (at which he took his father's place), the Sunday School classes and meetings and other church activities. There were classes, lectures, debates, clubs, excursions, and political meetings, parties for croquet (afternoon) and parlour games (evening). There are many entries of 'awfully busy all day', which refer to office work, but by getting up before breakfast and sitting up late at night, the real work of his life was squeezed in.

AUG. 13, 1874. Opened bottles, cats, snakes, and specimens of annulosa and annelids etc. a delightful odour in my room. emptied out some preparations I did not want and got old and empty bottles cleaned—spread open the slugs, sea cucumber etc. and pinned out insects scorpions etc.

[1] February 26, 1874: 'I find it harder to study veg. than animals by myself. It is pretty easy to understand by reading.'

14th. did about the same both before breakfast and after I came home. Rebottled my cobra. did tree frog etc. etc. cut my finger in the middle of it all and did not know it. washed it well, when found no evil consequences. before breakfast dissected a small banded fish.

15th. Bought a thin bullock's bladder for 4*d*. and more spirits at 10*d*. per lb. Worked hard all afternoon and before breakfast, got a headache and turned my room into a heaven below. it is glorious to see nature all around me. all classes of animals are thus subject to me illustrating the command to subject all unto myself. After tea went to the Adams' to take the object glass but could not get the thing to show at all clearly. Nailed up some wall fruit trees for them and played with the little ones. a bad headache but I did not care at all. I went on and chatted and in the end gave them a sort of impromptu lecture on cuttlefish etc.

In spite of cutting a wisdom tooth, toothache, earache and headaches he had 'a lovely day' at the Crystal Palace with the stuffed animals ('a pet idea of mine worked out'), and the next day spent 'a pleasant evening' with Grandma Haddon.

We read part of Prof. Tyndall's opening speech of the Brit. Ass. very interesting. it gave me an idea. All senses are more or less modifications of touch.

Towards the time of the family's return 'Tidied my room before breakfast'; 26th and 27th, 'Tidied again'; and on the 28th

They all came home. It quite deluged me. They brought me a great many curiosities, pieces of rocks, ores, etc. I am quite satisfied. Ma and Pa gave me a serpentine breast pin, Edie and Laura a pair of sleeve links.

The headaches continued.

Head hot and stuffy. In evening set to and wrote out all the story about wasps and read it to E. and L. They liked it the best and I worked so hard that my headache could not make itself felt till I had finished. You can't cheat nature.

Next day 'felt better, but at times stuffy sensation came on—especially when thinking of business'.

Thinking of business induced not only stuffy sensations, but actual repugnance; the boy's whole heart and soul were devoted to science, he felt himself a square peg in a round hole and saw stretching out before him a vista of a life of incompetence. There were complaints that he was careless and slipshod, both in the work itself and in money matters. When he had been left in charge during his father's absence he recorded his enjoyment of the importance of unrestrained authority, though his enjoyment was perhaps tempered by the receipt of terse and underlined letters from his father demanding to know why certain instructions had not been carried out.

This period of frustration, however unsatisfactory, was not altogether unprofitable for his life work. In spite of his lack of interest the boy learnt business methods and the importance of order and regularity. His familiarity with printing processes, type setting and proof reading stood him in good stead, and when correcting his own proofs it gave him unfeigned pleasure—rarely achieved— to detect an inverted *s* or an inconsistent cap. in the meticulous output of the Cambridge University Press. He also learnt, or evolved for himself, labour-saving methods in the preservation and filing of correspondence, so that in the apparent confusion of his littered desk he was always able to put his hand on the required paper and nothing was really mislaid.

The office was Duty and Drudgery. Outside the office he took an eager interest in almost everything. Besides the classes in drawing and designing, and lessons in copper-plate etching in preparation for his printing career, he attended evening classes at King's College, where lectures on Comparative Anatomy and Zoology were being given by Prof. Garrod; and at Birkbeck College, where Dr Carpenter was lecturing on Geology ('I knew before pretty well all I heard', October 24, 1874).

He joined scientific, pseudo-scientific and debating societies and took a course of lessons in Elocution.

He was an ardent member of the Y.M.C.A., acting on the Executive Committees, reading papers on *Microscopical Pond Life* and leading a discussion on *Phrenology: Does it reveal Character?*

I spoke impromptu (con) for abt 15 min. or 20. I am not really con and argued that the medical profession were. Drew diagrams of the brain on the blackboard (March 17, 1874).

The next paper was on the extent of the deluge, a very controversial subject when evolution was still a stumbling block in religious circles, and Darwinism was equated with atheism.

Mr E. read a very good paper. I spoke and drew a diagram of the country about Syria and showed that salt lakes are a peculiarity of that part of the world. Mr R. spoke and made an ass of himself and I got up and told him so. His knowledge of geology is nil.

Neither lessons in Elocution, nor years of painful practice, ever made him a good or fluent speaker. His father had a noticeable impediment in his speech, and as his family grew up they shuddered when he rose to speak

14

at a meeting and were thankful when he sat down. Still he said what he intended to say, fearless of criticism and careless of opposition. His son had something of his father's hesitancy, and all of his courage. He said what he meant to say, his ideas tripping over each other in their haste, with bursts of eloquence and patches of stuttering jerks, which were sometimes more effective than eloquence. As a lecturer, those who shared his enthusiasms found him inspiring; those who did not often found him wearisome. But there was usually some new comparison or deduction, some flash of wit or some happy turn of phrase to enliven the dreariest topics, and only the unimaginative could fail to be stimulated.

His first real experience of lecturing was at his aunts' school at Dover. This school was a remarkable experiment of which 'Aunt Carrie' was for many years the central inspiration.

Out of the total of thirteen children born to John Haddon and his wife between 1823 and 1842 only four, John (the father of A. C. H.), James, Wilberforce (named after the philanthropist), and Thomas, were boys. Two little girls died in infancy, but there were still seven lively and intelligent daughters to be educated and provided for, in the days when careers for girls were limited.

Education was the first concern and the elder pair, Marianne and Margaret, when only twelve and ten years old, were sent all the way to Manchester to school, taking two days on the journey. Later they went to a school in London and Marianne 'finished' in Paris. She, being the eldest, helped to teach her younger sisters, but the home education was interrupted as the doctor attributed a succession of sore throats to the smoky atmosphere of London and advised her living elsewhere. A summer holiday at Dover provided the solution. A small house was taken there in 1847 and Marianne and Margaret, then aged twenty-one and twenty, became the mistresses, while Elizabeth, Caroline and Charlotte were the pupils, and made the nucleus of the school. Other children soon joined them and they added house to house and flourished for forty years. Margaret married first, Marianne some years later, and still later Charlotte, but by that time the younger sisters were able to carry on the tradition, and it was Caroline who raised the school to the front rank among the pioneering girls' schools of the day.

Natural Science, particularly geology, was taught from the first, and A. C. H. saw in this an excellent chance of getting some practice in public speaking. He wrote to suggest a course of lectures on Geology and Zoology, which his aunt readily approved, and he started with an audience of about fifteen girls (March 2, 1874). His comment is 'I believe it was pretty successful'. The next lecture was his favourite one that he had already given to the Young Men's Christian Association on Microscopic Pond Life. This was a busy day (March 10, 1874). He was staying with Aunt Marianne at Ewell, some three miles out of Dover.

Read to Aunt, Darwin's *Emotions*. walked to Dover, got a bottle of weed as I went along. went and had a warm sea bath after lunch. gave a lecture on Microscopic Pond Life to about 17 girls. Had dinner. gave another lecture to abt 12 girls. Had tea. went to lecture on Light and Shadows of London Life by Mr McCree.

With the envious comment 'He had extreme self-assurance'.

After the last lecture of the course

Aunt gave me £1 in parting but I shall not accept it for it is not a fair recompence. a quarter would have been ample. I went to improve myself more than anything else.[1]

He showed his gratitude by acting as 'Universal Aunt' to the school girls.

Aunt Carrie writes:

I must ask a favour of you... Maude Robertson has to visit her grandmother on Saturday, could you manage to meet her at 3.25 p.m. at Ludgate Hill and put her in the omnibus. I suppose the Eagle for Camden Town would be the best... I must leave that to you. You would find her waiting in the ladies' room.

He had his reward later:

If you can spare time to run in to Ludgate Hill Station at 1.20 tomorrow, you will see no end of young ladies, a few *Melicerta* and *Stephanoceros,* and *Floscularia* in profusion, also the long-armed *Hydra* and two or three varieties of *Vorticella.* These precious treasures are in a bottle and will be handed to you by one of the aforesaid young ladies, Gertrude Lake, if you will show yourself when the Dover train arrives. She will know you if you do not know her.

One may guess that this would be a more congenial job than convoying Maude Robertson across London, but the aunt sympathises with her shy nephew:

I daresay it will be somewhat of an ordeal for you to face so

---

[1] 'Haddon never cared about money', as Sir Arthur Shipley said on the occasion of his 70th birthday, and his friends described him as 'without money and without price'.

many of the 'opposite sect' but for the sake of the long-armed *Hydra* what sacrifice is too great?

The 'opposite sect' was not objected to; there are indeed complacent entries 'I was the only gent' at evening parties, and parties are very frequent in the diaries, church membership being the connecting link and the large families of that date providing abundant companionship. The social recreations included croquet in the summer, whist, bagatelle or billiards in the winter, but the usual entertainments were parlour games, especially charades and moods (guessing an adverb by the tone of answers to questions) and such-like games, depending on intelligence rather than on chance.

FEB. 6, 1874. Had first-class evening at Adams', talk, charades, Bone-eye-face [zoology intrudes even here]...I thoroughly enjoy evenings like this. No humbug.

The interpretation of 'humbug' may be seen in the entry about the valentines sent with generous impartiality to each of the six Adamses 'Sensible with no sickly sentimental love-rot'.

These social evenings were expected to be 'profitable' as well as enjoyable and the talks are emphasised more than the games. There are constant references to 'nice talks' on Instinct, 'On some of the reasons why in this world', on religious philosophy, on political economy, on Man's place in nature and Darwinism.

But parties were sometimes disappointing:

MAY 29, 1874. Visitors to tea, played billiards, moods, etc. rather a dull evening, I don't think I got one new truth. Was it a wasted evening?

18

Later on dancing is added to evening entertainments, but he has no illusions about his proficiency:

SEPT. 29, 1874. Went in evening to Adams'. I was just in time to act in a charade, then we danced, even I! And had a good lot of it too. Had a pleasant evening.

At a party at home 'danced with my usual elegance!' Or 'Just danced or made a muddle of it, to please Katie'.

Shortly after this his sister Laura takes him to dancing classes. 'I am decidedly clumsy' is his comment, and his sister remembers how he nearly landed the teacher on the floor (January 18, 1875).[1]

Neither Alfred nor his sister had any ear for music and they found any but round dances more anxiety than enjoyment. John Haddon, their father, and John Haddon, their grandfather, were both distinguished musicians and both did good service in raising the standard of music and especially of hymn-singing in Baptist chapels. John Haddon, grandfather, brought out *The Psalmist* and *The New Selection Hymnbook*; his son published several psalm and hymn-books among which the *Wesleyan Hymn Book* is the best known. But musical talent failed in the next generation. Laura recalls her trials at Sunday School, when she was unable to start the children's hymn on the right note, and how when she and her brother went to the Moody and Sankey revivals, an impatient enthusiast behind thumped Alfred on the back with the objurgation, 'Sing, man, sing!'

[1] It was lucky that there was no clumsiness at the dance in Wild Gun's painted lodge among the Blackfeet of Montana in which he took a prominent part in 1909, as any mishap on that occasion would have been regarded as an evil omen (cf. p. 135).

19   2-2

All this time A. C. H. entered whole-heartedly into the religious life of the community. His parents were leading lights of Nonconformity and the children as a matter of course taught in the Sunday Schools and attended the prayer meetings, while sermons from Mr Spurgeon or revivalist meetings of Moody and Sankey marked the red-letter days. Part of all this, especially the Sunday School teaching, was Duty with a capital D which ruled the Haddon household, but much of it was sincerely enjoyed. 'Very nice meeting', 'Enjoyed it very much', 'Liked it immensely' often follow reports of services or prayer meetings, and when he was enjoying a rare holiday at Matlock all by himself he attended the Congregational Church in the morning and the United Wesleyans in the evening in spite of being thoroughly tired out. Doubts creep in occasionally, as at the Sunday School teachers' meeting, 'Very windy. Not much better sometimes than old maids'; and a prayer meeting may be 'not very interesting' and even 'a failure', followed by 'think I shall give it up'.

There is a significant entry recording a meeting with Mr W. W. Gill, the missionary from the South Seas, which may have been one of the first links with that part of the world which he was to make peculiarly his own. He describes him as 'the only man I have yet met who is in complete harmony with me' (May 15, 1875). The clue to the 'complete harmony' is found in a letter written by Mr Gill many years later (November 30, 1888) when inviting the explorer to visit him in New South Wales after his first sojourn in Torres Straits. 'I take a pride in recollecting my prophecy of your future eminence, not in business but in natural science.' Both meetings were momentous. The first strengthened Haddon's determination to devote himself to science rather than business; the second encouraged him to turn from Zoology to Anthropology (p. 90).

The diaries might have the subtitle 'Zoology Self-taught', as every opportunity is seized and nothing dissectible is wasted. Books were too expensive to buy and difficult to borrow, so all the more dependence was placed on practical experiment, ducks and hens, rabbits and moles, rats and tortoises all assisting in the work.

The dissection of the first tortoise, that 'died from cause unknown', was troublesome and not very successful. The next was worse. 'Found dead tortoise. Smelt horribly. shell awfully hard to open. gave my finger a bad cut. had to use poker.' Kittens were simpler and all the neighbours' drowned kittens were collected. Also dead hens.

Here is a typical Saturday afternoon (March 28, 1874):

Walk with Edith and Laura in Park and woods. enjoyed myself immensely. Got a great many primroses. I took Mrs Tumner some. picked up a smashed hedgehog. called at Adams' for dead hen. had a game of billiards and dissected hen with Willie. died probably from a blow, perhaps a stick. I think I found a piece of wood inside it. Splendid hen.

The most delightful jumble is recorded in April (1872):

Guinea-pigs born. the blackbirds have left the nest [there had been daily notes and sketches of the blackbird fledgelings for the week before]. Went to Congregational Sunday School for examination. Put It is sown in dishonour, it riseth in glory on the illumination. on the under side of tadpoles there is an oval nearly transparent hole and you see something like viscera of a greyish colour. the hind legs have begun to come. my newt has left the water in the last day or two and looks very bad.

Making, stocking and studying the insectarium and aquarium take up most of the spare time. Besides the tadpoles and newts there were smaller and smaller creatures, and as time goes on more and more space is given to the microscope and its revelations, with notes of structures and behaviours illustrated by minute sketches. 'Showed microscope' is the usual entry whenever visitors come to the house, with comments that they 'seemed interested', or 'F. does not seem interested—F. is a duffer'. There are also public exhibitions and occasionally rare bits of luck.

APRIL 16, 1874. Cleaned microscope and thought what object I should exhibit. I chose Morpho Menelaus but felt uneasy about it as that is merely a beautiful object and does not teach much.

The very next day comes the letter from Aunt Carrie already quoted (p. 17) saying that she is sending him a bottle of treasures.

Just what I was longing for. Met the girls. got the bottle, went to Thornthwaites and bought a zoophyte trough to exhibit them in. Went to the Quekett Soirée and shewed them. they all came out beautifully.

Before we leave the diaries one more day must be quoted as it is marked in capitals.

FIRST DAY OUT OF ENGLAND IN MY LIFE

and a busy day it was too. He was staying at Folkestone with the Walkers.

AUG. 14, 1875. Willie, Louie and I went by 9.10 steamer to Boulogne. got there abt 11.30. without being at all seasick. changed 10/-. went to N. side of town to cliffs, got a piece of the rock, back by sands, into town to museum, into Notre Dame and old crypt, had dinner, a walk into country and to the column, made 3 sketches. over another church, through the gardens of the Tintilleries. coffee at a restaurant. walked along the quay. home at 9. rough sea especially coming home. enjoyed myself immensely.

Letters of this period, fortunately preserved, throw light on its main interests. They are all 'very animally' as his sister describes them:

I am afraid it will not be possible to get a live mantis to you because they are very short-lived (from Aunt Charlotte, Colombo).

I am sorry I cannot tell you the size of a cat's stomach (Donald Ferguson).

The rotifera you left for me in the cup for examination had absconded. will you tell me how and where to get some more? (from a fellow Millhillian).

In a schoolboy letter from cousin Harry Waterman, written in daily sections interspersed with objurgations of Caesar and cancelled half holidays:

Have you dissected any more unfortunate mouse, rat or cat that you may happen to come across? I am sure I pity them with all my heart.... Today is Sunday so I cannot write much as I do not think it is right to write letters on Sunday except when it is absolutely necessary. Have you had any more skulls given you?

Two more letters may be quoted to illuminate this period. One is from a contemporary who writes to thank for a 'kind thoughtful letter' full of good wishes and advice, emphasising the importance of '*continually striving after knowledge*'. The friend quotes, as summing up the gist of the letter:

> Fill up each hour with what will last,
> Buy up the moments as they go,
> The life above, when this is past,
> Is the ripe fruit of life below.

The eager 'striving after knowledge' and the generous desire to share his knowledge and to inspire others with the same enthusiasms were as characteristic at this stage as throughout his life.

The other letter is from his mother written early in 1873. He had written to say that he wanted to join the Quekett Microscopical Club (10s. a year), also that he intended to join the [Baptist] church. The order in which the two desires are placed is significant, as is also his mother's reply:

I am glad to hear that you intend joining the Quekett Society as I think you will be gaining good by it. I daresay the needful expenses can be met.

Then come motherly admonitions about personal appearance:

Keep yourself personally smart. Take a pride in your hands, hair and nails.... Because you do not care for outward appearance it does not follow that you are therein right.... It wants determination and patience with you even to wash your hands as often as you ought to do. Now never give in. You want more doggedness about you.

That seems to her more important than the Quekett Society, but there is something more important still and the subject she really wants to write about, his desire to be 'planted in the house of the Lord', fills the next two pages. One or two extracts may be given:

Science and culture have their place but they are not necessarily spiritual, and it is the spiritual world that matters.

She writes a long and beautiful exposition of the text 'Ye *must* be born again':

We know that we are sinful, weak, foolish, that we are bankrupt in goodness, that we stand in awful future peril, and that our moral nature needs reconstructing....

God teaches the willing soul according to its willingness to be taught...he goes on year after year till more and more we bear the image of the heavenly; and the soul at all hours, in all circumstances, instinctively turns to the invisible but felt presence of God. So we abide in him, so our daily life is lived by his side, so we walk with God. Communion with God is a very need of living. The world is a blank without God. The cause dear to him is dear to us. His foes are ours, and we must be co-workers together with God. His honour must be dearer than our own. He must come *first*.

This was the revelation to the mother and she lived in the presence of her God. That to the son was through a different medium. A selfless and passionate devotion to Science came first, leading to the revelation of a more universal but less scriptural deity, and with this devotion no accepted conventions, religious or social, could be allowed to interfere.

The account of crowded days contained in the diaries

does not suggest much leisure, but somehow time was found for writing, which met with beginners' luck.

Marlborough Chapel in Old Kent Road issued a *Monthly Magazine* and the publishers were Messrs Hutchings of 5 Bouverie Street, close to the Haddon office. In 1874 the magazine inaugurated a series of prize competitions calculated to improve the mind:

Having regard to the advanced intelligence and superior culture of our readers, we do not invite them to decipher hieroglyphics, nor to discover 'buried cities', nor to construct 'square words', nor to interpret 'anagrams', 'charades', or 'conundrums'. We prefer to test their attainments in various branches of scientific knowledge, taking Geology as a commencement.

A chart of the *Development of the Earth's Crust* was given, and a prize offered in books to the value of one guinea for the best interpretation, with descriptions, of flora and fauna.

The annotations of the chart by the future anthropologist give evidence of the industry of the self-taught geologist; they reflect the advanced, but still orthodox opinion of the day, interpreted in the language of the Marlborough Chapel connection, but they give no hint of future greatness.

In the earliest eons of the world's existence, life was not; all was darkness and unintelligible arrangement, though not confusion; for He 'whose Almighty word, Chaos and darkness heard, and took their flight' could never be disorderly, for 'Order is heaven's first law'. Gigantic forces were groaning and travailing together, working out under fixed laws the will of God, which was the preparation for an orderly world, in which He might manifest Himself.

Homo does not manifest himself earlier than in the post-Glacial post-Pliocene period, when he appears as a semi-clothed savage dwelling in caves or in houses built on piles and hunting the mammoth.

'Adamic Man' appears in Surface Soil,

made up of leaves and decaying vegetable mould—wearing down of rocks—remains of our forefathers who were not cremated—in fact the soil on which we walk. Adamic Man by divine command subdues the forces of nature, improves or exterminates all the brute creation, including by a mysterious Providence even his less favoured brethren, but he himself is not himself. The Ego is merely connected with the Homo in order by the necessary sufferings, trials and pains, to render him who 'for a little while was made lower than the angels' a fit receptacle for the unspeakable love of God.

This essay won the first prize, which was spent on Nicholson's *Manual of Palaeontology* and Maunder's *Treasury of Natural History*.

Other efforts were less successful. *Foolish Fancies by a Frenzied Philosopher* was certainly copied out and sold (or offered) at 2*s*. 6*d*. a copy at a church bazaar, but such stray MSS. as *On the Hearthrug*, or *On the Art of Dying*, were probably intended for a literary club, not for publication. *Adventures among the Water-babies* is more characteristic, describing and illustrating his favourite 'beasties'. There is a lively water flea who saves the life of the author, itself to be swallowed up by a terrifying hydra 'looking just as if someone had tied half the bodies of a number of snakes together and left the head-halves to writhe about after the most approved serpentine fashion'.

27

There was an essay on the *Circulation of Love* and *Creation of Man* with a little more of Darwin and less of Marlborough Chapel. The family reactions are described by his sister Laura who spent several hours in copying the MS.

Father's criticism was 'Oh Yes', and when I pressed further said he 'would think about it'. Mamma said ditto, but thought it a wee bit too dogmatic, that it raised a lot of questions, that you had good ideas, and finally that it reminds her of the image in Nebuchadnezzar's dream which was part gold, part silver, iron, clay, etc. Edie can make or see neither head nor tail in it.

Half Hours with the Insects was returned with polite regrets by publisher after publisher. Marcus Ward, though regretful, holds out hopes: 'Could you however favour us with a call—our Editor will be here and would be happy to give you some hints which if carried out might be of use to you' (December 1874).

This editor was a man of some critical discrimination, but even he could scarcely have guessed that this young literary aspirant would come to be reckoned as one of the most brilliant contributors to the *Daily Chronicle* at its zenith (cf. p. 130), or that his literary output in the course of the next half-century would run into some six hundred items (p. 153). He offered to consider stories about birds, but by this time preparation for Cambridge had already started and the offer was not accepted.

All these years the square peg had been fretting more and more in its round hole, seeking everywhere for a way of escape, answering advertisements, applying for posts, asking everywhere for information and advice and receiving nothing but discouragement.

This was no secret from the family, all the uncles and aunts and grandparents seem to have been taken into his confidence, and from their letters of condolence we learn something of the lions in the path of a scientific career in those days.

As early as 1872 he had written to Professor Owen, superintendent of the Natural History Collection in the British Museum (a favourite haunt of the young zoologist), and received a courteous but disappointing reply, advising the boy to stick to his job, *as there was no hope of his earning a living in a scientific career*.

Grandfather Waterman knowing that 'the bent of your mind was so strongly set and the current of your thoughts were almost absorbed in your favourite pursuit' writes to sympathise:

> As such pursuits are almost in their very nature unproductive excepting to a favoured few—and those who have resources to fall back upon, I hope that these considerations will help you to bear your disappointment with fortitude, and hope that all this even will turn out for the best, and believe that a kind Providence will provide an opening for your well-being in some other sphere. . . . Try to like and pursue any respectable occupation which may, with God's blessing be for your present or future welfare.

Other correspondents were equally discouraging but some made more helpful suggestions.

Aunt Charlotte and Uncle John Ferguson of Colombo had sent their nephew various specimens packed in with books and papers such as insects (including a queen termite) and snakes (including a cobra), and in his letter of thanks he had lamented that he knew no man of tastes

29

similar to his own whom he could call a friend. Aunt Charlotte sent him an introduction to Mr Ambrose Fleming who had recently been appointed science master at Cheltenham College. He lost no time in following up this new opening and wrote describing his attraction to science and repugnance to the office, both of which were growing stronger and stronger as time went on.

Mr Fleming begins by regretting that the scientific attraction is for Geology and Physiology instead of Chemistry and Physics, which have more practical and utilitarian value, and points out that there is no intermediate stage between an *amateur* and a *Professor*.

Of course Geology is essential to a mining engineer and Physiology to a medical man. But apart from this I know of no way by which any one could make a living out of them except by teaching; and even for this teaching there is but a limited demand...and the candidates are many, and a long and expensive education added to great natural talents are essential.

He suggests the possibility of turning Geology to practical use as a mining engineer, with the three years' course at the Royal School of Mines; or, if Physiology is more attractive, of becoming a doctor:

But I confess myself at a complete loss to know how to point out any way by which you could out of Geology or Physiology earn an income 'sufficient to keep a wife'....I am afraid you will consider this very chilling advice.

But he ends with the happy prediction 'Feeling sure that if you are bent on embracing a scientific career, some opportunity will turn up for you some time'.

A letter in the *Spectator* advocating the endowment of scientific research led to correspondence with the writer,

C. E. Appleton of *The Academy*. He—an Oxford man—points out that the only chance of endowment is through Oxford or Cambridge, and advises the boy to go to Oxford

where you can now live as an unattached student for £50 a year. Stay 3 years, take the modicum of classics required and try to distinguish yourself in Natural History and cognate sciences, in which you will find excellent helpers in Prof. Rolleston, Prof. Westwood and Mr E. Ray Lankester. By the time you are ready there will probably be at least a Fellowship to be won—but if the Conservative Government take up the Endowment of Research, it is quite possible that you may get some such post as I have tried to sketch in the *Spectator*.

The real significance of this letter lies, as often happens, in the P.S.

If you prefer Cambridge you will find there the Ornithologist, Prof. Newton and the Physiologist, Dr Michael Foster,[1] both first rate in their way.

And here again, an aunt comes to the rescue. This time it is Aunt Marianne Offord. She has read the letters from Mr Fleming and from Mr Appleton and she makes wise comments:

Naturally a doctor's education is most in harmony with your favorite pursuits but then there is the chemistry that stands barring the road unless your ideas on that point have changed since last year.... As for the University, Is your antipathy to

[1] Alfred Newton was the first Professor of Zoology at Cambridge, 1866–1907. Michael Foster was Praelector of Physiology at Trinity and had just published his *Elements of Embryology*. Huxley and he were then revolutionising the teaching of science by their insistence on practical work.

Latin the effect of ignorance or does it arise from something in your mind altogether antipathetic to the study of a language— I fancy not. You did not make much use of school advantages in that line, I believe, but perhaps you were stupidly taught, so that your faculties were really never engaged in it and now with your *man's* intellect you might succeed well.

Then comes the definite suggestion:

Suppose you quickly tested this for 3 months at home. I cannot imagine how you can be a scientist without a tolerable knowledge of Latin, and an amateur you dont *want* to be.... your chief hindrance seems to me to arise from a sort of intellectual wilfulness. Do you know what I mean? Your likes and dislikes stand in the way of wide culture.

She quotes Kirke White who said that because he suspected himself of disliking mathematics he gave it special attention, and adds, 'Excuse this preaching [no other relatives ever said that], I daresay your own observation says the same thing.'

Far more important than the 'preaching' is the introduction to S. S. Lewis[1] in Cambridge. Anxious to leave no stone unturned A. C. H. had probably hunted out all the Professors whose names Appleton had given him, and Aunt Marianne remembers having known Michael Foster as a lad. Now she writes:

I have had some talk about you these last days as I have had a Cambridge Fellow staying here. He is a friend of Dr Michael Foster and would be happy to see you at Cambridge any day between the 7th and 20th Jan. [1875] and introduce you to Dr Foster and the other great natural science man there, and

[1] Rev. Samuel Savage Lewis, 1836–91. Fellow and Librarian of Corpus Christi College, collector of coins and gems.

tell you in connection with what colleges you would have the best chance of a fellowship.... he asks if your principles are settled so that you could safely go to one of the smaller colleges without wasting your time on billiards etc. as they are colleges to be avoided for youths of unsettled habits. I tell him there is no fear of your being diverted by sports of any kind. He [Mr Lewis] is one who determinately sets before him as his part to help undergraduates in their studies and not in their sports. His own pursuit is antiquities and he also preaches a good deal in villages round.

Here was a blaze of hope and the introduction to Cambridge sealed the boy's fate. His father had long ago realized that he could never make a business man of him and said ruefully that though he could not afford it he would lose less money by sending him to the University than by keeping him in the office, and he had written to Dr Michael Foster asking his advice as to the chance of making a livelihood by training in science. The answer fills two sheets and is perfectly frank.

At the present moment [November 27, 1874] the life of a scientific man is a very hard and unremunerative one. He can only get money by teaching or lecturing or writing and even then with such difficulty that very little time is left for original research. Were there no chance of things being altered I would strongly advise your son to remain a publisher and devote his leisure to science as has been done by so many distinguished men.... Should chances in favour of natural science and research be soon made there would then be openings which do not exist now and men at the University would most probably get decent livelihoods with opportunities for inquiry. But this is quite *contingent* no one can say whether changes of such a kind will be made and still less when.

You see my difficulty...and how one is prevented from giving any decided advice....I would not advise his entering the medical profession. He would have far more leisure as a publisher....Any other information that I can give you will be a pleasure to me and I should be very happy to see your son if, after this letter, you still think it advisable to send him down.

Mr Haddon decided that the risk was worth taking and he advertised for a tutor to prepare his son for the Previous Examination for Cambridge. So A. C. H. left the hated office 'for a time' and turned to the equally uncongenial Latin, Greek and Maths., having lessons from the Rev. Mr Hunt, Chaplain Assistant at the Royal Hospital, Chelsea, often given in the vestry in the intervals between christenings and funerals.

The next point to be settled was the entry to a Cambridge College, and here again Michael Foster was appealed to:

I think on the whole I should advise you to go to Christ's. They are doing more for natural science there than in any other college. It would be either that or Caius—but on the whole Christ's. They are very liberal with their scholarships etc. and it is a good working college and the Fellows are for the most part liberal and sensible men.

After reviewing the attractions and disadvantages of Sidney Sussex, St John's and Downing 'Yes, I think Christ's is the best for you'.

Extracts from the diary for 1875 briefly record these stepping-stones to higher things:

JAN. 15, 1875. Awfully busy all day. Went to Kings College. Found classes did not begin till Monday. Learnt Greek alphabet. felt quite done up.

FEB. 1. Went to Mr Hunt's. Heard some Latin nouns, verbs etc. FIRST DAY OF MY NEW LIFE. CRISIS IN MY HISTORY HAS NOW TAKEN PLACE.

FEB. 9. Maths, algebra, Euclid.

MARCH 27th. Began Greek, Aristophanes. *Birds*. Took $1\frac{1}{2}$ hours a line!

MARCH 29th. Bank Holiday. Got up at 6.15. did $1\frac{1}{2}$ hours Greek before breakfast and $2\frac{1}{2}$ hours more in the day.

JUNE 1. did most Greek ever done in a day. 65 lines.

JUNE 8. Finished Aristophanes.

JUNE 9th. Began Greek Testament.

SEPT. 29. Last day with Mr Hunt.

OCT. 3. My last Sunday. Said Goodbye to lots of people.

OCT. 6. £30 for Cambridge from Pa.

OCT. 7. Went to Cambridge.

Chapter II

CAMBRIDGE

October 1875—*December* 1880

THERE is no BEGINNING OF MY NEW LIFE in capital letters to mark the first Thursday in October, 1875, when A. C. H. went up to Cambridge, and his first impressions were disappointing. The entries in his diary might serve the normal freshman of his, or of any other, year.

OCT. 7. Went to Cambridge by 12.15 train from King's Cross. Got there about 1.30. took a cab to my lodgings [15 Ely Place]. found my rooms occupied by Mr C. and F. who had had an accident. had to sleep in a very small upstairs room. had dinner with Mr C. Called on Mr Peile[1] [tutor] in evening. He gave me a list of the rules and told me what to do. bought my cap and gown.

OCT. 8. Began to settle. First day in Cambridge. not a nice town. straggling, no really nice houses. Christ's rather a disreputable looking College. Walked about. Went to Hall. Mr C. took me to the Union. Wrote home.

Saturday was the beginning of the preliminary examination for the Previous Examination which was taken very seriously and occupied the whole term. 'Started Little Go. Did the classic translations very well, the rest only moderately.'

[1] J. Peile, afterwards Master, 1887–1910.

On Sunday 'Went to Chapel [College chapels were compulsory] morning and evening. rather an unprofitable day.'

The next week he called on his tutor and the Master (J. Cartmell) and was excused all chapels henceforward: 'very kind and liberal men'. So the following Sunday was more 'profitable'.

Went to breakfast with Briggs[1] [a 3rd year Classic] very jolly. plenty of religious anecdotes etc. Then on to Congregational Chapel. nice service and good singing. a very handsome building.

Services at the Congregational Chapel which he formally joined (November 7) or at the Wesleyan Chapels in Hobson Street or Hills Road fill in the following Sundays of the term, and there were Bible readings and prayer meetings (with the usual comment 'very nice') in chapel or in students' rooms, especially those of J. B. Harrison, a fellow-freshman.

As usual the first contacts were due to propinquity and they were not altogether congenial. Mr C. was temporarily established in the rooms that should have been his and F. was 'the upstairs man'. He was much impressed with 'the upstairs man' at first: 'He is going in for Honours, Little Go and Science Tripos', which

---

[1] E. F. A. Briggs was Representative of the Society for the Liberation of Religion from State Patronage and Control, an office which he handed over to A. C. H. later (June 1878). He was a stimulating iconoclast and shocked the Haddon family when he came to stay with them by tilting against funeral ceremonies. 'He is the extreme mould of a reformer who would eliminate blacks for mourning', comments Aunt Marianne.

sounded big to a novice. But his name does not appear in the list of successful candidates for the Previous or reappear in the diaries.

With these stable-companions A. C. H. had his first wine. He went to tea with Mr C. and there met one of his friends 'who joked me on being a teetotaller', but there was also a Roman Catholic priest present 'who took my part, gave me good advice, felt my heart, said it was good enough for a Premier's'. That was on Wednesday. On Friday he was no longer a teetotaller.

Mr C. had a party and we had a wine! I had half a glass of champagne. jolly evening.

The next wine was not so enjoyable.

To K.'s after chapel to a wine. Took a glass of champagne. Left at 8. too dirty talk and silly humbug.

The next time Mr C. is mentioned it is at another wine, when he 'fell all to pieces and soon sank into a state of insensibility'; and the last mention is after 'an unprofitable evening' in the rooms of 'the upstairs man'. 'Mr C. left. Glad he is gone.'

Whether from choice or from necessity A. C. H. indulged neither in smoking nor in drinking in his undergraduate days. Before coming up to Cambridge a friend made a bet that he would 'take to the noxious weed and be drunk on the premises'—and lost the bet. But he started smoking a pipe when he was fifty, to please his wife, who missed the smell of tobacco in the house when their son, Ernest, went out to Uganda.

Soon there were more congenial companions. The beginning of a life-long friendship with Rendel Harris is dated by a Religious Equality meeting in his rooms in Clare (November 22, 1875) which was 'great' and 'lasted from 7.30 till past 11'.

A Bible reading was the occasion of the first meeting with Holland Rose with whom he was to be so closely connected for the next sixty-five years. They went together to hear Dr Asa Mahan preach. Rose came back to tea and they played chess together afterwards. Thenceforward there are many entries of 'walked with Rose. he came back to lunch', or 'Rose came in. played chess'. And at the end of the term, just before the dreaded Greek Grammar paper, a stumbling block to so many, 'Rose gave me a few tips'.[1]

This close friendship with Rose was curious as they seemed to have little besides Nonconformity in common. Rose was a classical scholar with no special interest in science or in 'beasties'; he was very fond of music and, possessing a good voice, enjoyed musical evenings which A.C.H. could not appreciate. He was an enthusiastic oarsman, having been trained at Bedford; he rowed in his College boat and spent much time on the river. In spite

[1] His sister Laura, the future Mrs Holland Rose, had also come to the rescue in his struggles with Greek grammar, learning the alphabet so that she could help him, but to this day she wonders how he ever got through the paper. He was surprised himself (though he noted that he did better than he expected), and when the news of his having passed was received on Christmas Eve there was as much astonishment as rejoicing in the family. Cf. Darwin's expression of his emotions after two years' preparation for the same examination at the same College, forty-five years earlier. He wrote, 'I am through, through, through, I could write the whole sheet full with this delightful word' (*Charles Darwin*, ed. F.D. 1902, p. 111).

of these preoccupations he soon recognised his fellow-freshman as 'one of the best' and they were constant companions on Sunday afternoon walks. They must have made an incongruous pair. Rose, the incipient school-master, with his almost classic features, his neat figure and short quick military step. Haddon, shabby, untidy, unkempt, striding along with the sprawliness and abandon of a lively puppy. But there was a fundamental similarity between them, for though pursuing different branches of knowledge their aims, methods and successes were the same. Each was eagerly searching after truth, and paid scrupulous attention to detail; yet both were capable of an unusually wide survey of the whole field, and A.C.H. doubtless owed much to Rose's maturer clarity and breadth of view.

Even Rose could not make A.C.H. into an oarsman. He had joined the Boat Club in his first week and ordered the regulation 'costume' from the College tailor (October 15); the next day he had his first tubbing: 'Had first attempt on the river for 15 minutes. did not get on very well.' The second attempt was the last, though he kept up his Boat subscription of £1. 1s. 0d. a term and helped to cheer his College boat on to victory from the towing path.

Rifle drill was a more agreeable form of exercise than rowing, and here again the 'costume' has to be ordered from the tailor. He enrolled in D Company of the Cambridge University Volunteers (October 22); ordered the 'rifle suit' on the 25th; had it fitted on the 28th; 'clothes came home', 30th; had first rifle drill in Trinity Paddock, November 1, 'Got on only pretty well.' However he 'passed the Adjutant' on November 20 and the culminating point comes on the 27th:

Company Dinner in Hall in uniform. Visitors in evening dress. After dinner a wine in [H. N.] Martin's rooms, lots of speeches etc. and some very good songs. broke up at 11. jolly evening. I only had 1 wineglass of claret and a sip or two of punch.

On December 1, the day of the Scratch Fours, 'First time I ever fired off a gun at all'. But his eye was good, he made 22 out of a possible 80, and at 300 yards 6 out of 20 was not too bad for a first attempt.

Apart from Holland Rose the companions of this first year at Cambridge were mainly Nat. Sci. men, and the names most frequently mentioned are those of W. H. Waters, William Collingridge, Walter Keeping and J. B. Harrison.

Waters and Haddon head the list of science scholars in the College examinations for the next two years, Waters, who had the advantage of an entrance scholarship, always leading. He was appointed Demonstrator in Physiology at Cambridge until 1882 when he went to Owens College, Manchester. His letters, signed H_2O, show that this friendship was kept up long after College days.

Collingridge[1] was a medical student with a love of adventure. He spent his first Long Vac. as volunteer surgeon in the Serbian army, then in the midst of the war against Turkey, and wrote interesting letters to A. C. H. describing his experiences.

[1] Afterwards Medical Officer of Health, Port of London and City of London.

41

Walter Keeping, afterwards Professor of Geology at Aberystwyth, was another fellow-freshman, who became a friend of the Haddon family. It was he who first introduced A. C. H. to the geological Museum and to Professor Hughes 'who was very enthusiastic and gave me a lot of good advice'.

Hughes had a great influence on Haddon as on all receptive students who caught his enthusiasm and took his advice. His insistence on field work, on carefully checked observations, on 'getting down to bed-rock'—no mere metaphor—and getting away from text-books, dominated Cambridge geology, and his application of the same technique to Cambridge archaeology in its early days helped to raise it from an amateur hobby to a science.

J. B. Harrison, in whose rooms weekly Bible readings and prayer meetings used to be held, was no namby-pamby type, and gave the College authorities some anxiety. He was also a geologist and did good work for the Geological Society of London in the West Indies and elsewhere before becoming Professor of Chemistry and Agricultural Science at Barbados and British Guiana. He made himself conspicuous in his first term, as A. C. H. notes in his diary.

On the Fifth of November there was

the usual town and gown row with great noise throughout the town but very little real riot at any time. I met a lot of Christ's men.

There was a worse row a few days later (November 8), nine men, including Harrison and another Christ's man, being sent to prison and bail refused. So the next night the mayor's effigy was burnt in the Market Place and there was 'another row. I went out at 8.40 but Mr Peile [tutor] sent me home....He got bail for our men.' The next day was 'the greatest row of all. The men were on trial and there was cheering as they appeared and a demonstration in front of the Guild Hall. The mayor [Mr Mortlock] spoke from a window....Harrison was imprisoned.' The next day the streets were quiet again, though there was a lot of excitement telling of deeds done the previous night.

No men about. Too well proctorised. I met Mr Peile as I was going to Mr Gross [out of college] and he told me not to be out late. Went to Mr Martin's rooms, saw Harrison there had a jolly time.

'Streets quiet. no row' describes the next day or so, and Bible readings and prayer meetings, though not in Harrison's rooms, end the week of excitement.

In those days very few undergraduates, and certainly none so ill-prepared for the University as A. C. H., could spare time for anything outside their own special subject even had they the inclination. They attended the lectures or classes advised by their tutors and rarely trespassed beyond. But A. C. H. was omnivorous and untiring, and his first excursions into other faculties showed the bias that influenced his whole life.

Cramming for the Previous both in Mathematics and in Classics was for him a really formidable task; entries in his diary show how seriously he regarded it, and at times he was in despair. In a fit of despondency he called on his tutor and explained his doubts and difficulties. Peile told him that he thought he had a chance of passing

43

if he had extra coaching and recommended Mr Gross of Caius. He hunted up Mr Gross and this leads to the first mention of G. Bettany of the same College (a useful literary adviser in later years), with whom he spent 'a very pleasant quiet evening, talking of science and art in general'. The two did not part before an appointment was made to go together to the lectures of Sidney Colvin (who was then Slade Professor of Fine Art) at the Fitzwilliam Museum, and there are appreciative comments on the course throughout the term.

That was not the only excursion into other departments. Although the Michaelmas term was ostensibly filled up with lectures and coaching for the Previous, Natural Science was always breaking in. There were hours spent in Museums, the Anatomical ('very fair. Museum too dark, some splendid model sets. good collection of skulls etc.'); the Geological Museum, also very dark in its cramped quarters in the Old Schools; and the Botanic Garden ('very nice collection, nice palms, also carnivorous plants'); and there were geological excursions to the chalk pits to collect fossils. Best of all were the pilgrimages to the top of Shelford Hill to call on Dr Michael Foster and talk Physiology.

Unfortunately the diaries end at Christmas 1875, so the rest of the Cambridge period has to depend mainly on what can be gleaned from stray letters and from College bills.

The bills of 1875–8 look strangely familiar. Coffee, tea, cocoa, sugar, jam, marmalade, sardines and biscuits are inevitable; eggs (then 1*d*. each), ham, tongue and tinned salmon (anticipating his favourite stand-by on the

Fly River), apples, oranges and dates may be found on any undergraduate bill of to-day. The bedmaker orders her ample stores of firewood, black lead, matches and soap, but adds the unfamiliar items of 'best Chrystal', dips, 'composites' and spills.

These bills bear evidence of careful economy and there are no extras before the Lent term of 1877, and then there is a burst. Coffee for seven occurs two days running, with toast and rolls (2s. 8d.), sixteen knives and forks (hired at 2s.) and two spoons (1½d.). A week later there is coffee for ten (5s.). Toast and rolls come to 3s.; there are twenty-two knives and forks and again inadequate spoons (four at 3d.). The pie and salmon bought at the grocer's the previous week suggest the purpose of the knives and forks, and though there is no evidence one may hazard the guess that these provisions were not laid out for private entertainment, but that in those days as in these, breakfasts were combined with Committee Meetings.

Easter term had its special attractions.

College and other examinations, for one brief week in this 'bonnie month of May' are forgotten in the delirious excite-ment of boat-races, concerts, fêtes and—ladies. We have as yet been unable to discover whether the ladies come to see the races or the races take place to please the ladies. Anyhow our fair visitors throng every evening to the river side to see their relations, real or intended, contest for aquatic honours, and Ditton Corner especially is gay with 'Mayflowers'.... On Wednesday the 17th the races began. The second division rowed soon after 6 p.m. Then the first division followed. This continued till the Saturday following, but on Monday and Tuesday, only the first division rowed.... After all the racing is over—on Thursday the 25th—the boats row in procession past the backs of the Colleges in the order of their place on the river decked with foliage, flowers and flags. Then they return and stop opposite King's College, when they, with interlocked rowlocks, form a closely-packed bright band across the river ...standing in the boats, holding up the oars, waving their hats...cheering [and drinking the health of] the Head of the River, and all the boats in succession.

This extract forms the beginning of a short article 'Cambridge in the May Term' which A.C.H. sent to the *Pictorial World*, with pictures of College gates and bridges surrounding two original sketches of 'Bumping at Ditton Corner' and 'The Boat Procession'.[1]

The next year's May Week was still more exciting, and the description of 'fair visitors, coming to see their relatives real *or intended*' has a personal application. The friendship with Holland Rose had continued and intensified, and for the May Week festivities of 1877 the two arranged to exchange sisters, Holland devoting himself to the lively and attractive Laura, while A.C.H. entertained Holland's quieter sister Fanny. The sister-exchange, which was suggested more or less as a joke, had

[1] These were published in the issue of June 3, 1876, and he received a cheque for £1. 1s. 0d. in return. The two original sketches were reissued fifty years later in the May Week number of *The Cambridge Review* for June 15, 1926, with recollections of the procession of boats (abandoned in 1893) by Dr H. Bond, Master of Trinity Hall. He was coxing the Trinity Hall boat in the May Week that A.C.H. describes, and he could still remember how difficult it was to steer through St John's, Trinity and Clare Bridges with a large full Moselle cup between his knees, without spilling it. 'The obvious solution of drinking the cup down to safety level before getting to St John's met with loud remonstrances from the crew.'

serious consequences. Holland Rose and Laura Haddon were engaged before the end of the year. They were married in the summer of 1880 and on the day of the wedding (August 5) A. C. H. announced his engagement to Fanny Rose. 'Never mind, I have brought you another daughter', he said to his mother. Other relatives made the same remark. Her sister-in-law (Mrs Edward Waterman) writes to Mrs Haddon from Clifton:

I well remember Alf telling me a droll tale about the compact he and Holland mutually entered into to look at each others sisters and see whether they liked them sufficiently to exchange etc. How Holland was smitten and at once succumbed. 'But about yourself and your part of the bargain?' I asked. But the story ended by his telling me that matrimony would certainly not enter his thoughts for years to come, till he had roamed into unknown regions....'Fanny?' 'Yes, Fanny was a nice girl enough', but not for him, he was married to beasties and birds and reptiles etc. etc. And now comes the news that this learned and grave Professor is taken captive!...Well dear, you will not I feel sure in the face of all this look for *condolences*, why, Carrie, you are fast growing rich in sons and daughters....

But Mrs Haddon did not see it at all in the same light. Fond as she was of her daughter-in-law to be, she could not help feeling (like any mother of a specially devoted son) that she was now losing a son as well as a daughter.

This is to anticipate. But in retracing his Cambridge career one may note that, to use his own phrase, 'there was always a petticoat in the offing',[1] and the necessity

---

[1] Sometimes there were three at once, as he complains in a letter to a friend, linking this 'disaster' with two others, i.e. opening pits in a British village and finding nothing, and two wet days at Stonehenge.

for earning a living sufficient to support a wife, even one so ready to share poverty with her husband as was Fanny Rose, became an ever-increasing anxiety which was never really allayed for a score of years to come.

The Previous Examination was conquered somehow by Christmas 1875. Physics and Chemistry had to be taken the following year, both entirely new subjects, to which Botany (Dr Vines), Geology (Dr Bonney), Anatomy and Physiology (Mr Balfour and Dr Foster) were added for the Honours course. Dr Vines commended him as 'a diligent student' especially successful in the physiology of plants; Dr Bonney described him as a most enthusiastic student of geology, eager in his pursuit of knowledge and thorough in his study; but his chief subjects were Anatomy and Physiology under Balfour and Foster, and for both of these teachers he had great admiration.

It was largely owing to Foster that Cambridge science was placed on a secure basis by the introduction of practical and experimental work and the insistence on observance of facts rather than acquaintance with theories. This just suited A.C.H. with his life-long distrust of 'brain-spinning' and constant demand for personal experiment. Foster's influence, both as a lecturer and as a friend, did much to accentuate these predilections, to confine accepted beliefs to those based on personal observation, and, incidentally, to weaken those which had no tangible foundation.

Another stimulating influence was that of F. M. Balfour (younger brother of Arthur J.), whose brilliant lecture notes were laying the foundations of his *Comparative Embryology* published a year or so later.

All his pupils seem to have fallen under his spell. This is the impression he made on H. F. Osborne[1] in 1879:

Never shall I forget my first impression of Francis Maitland Balfour as I met him in the great court of Trinity College of Cambridge in the spring of 1879, to apply for admission to his course in embryology. At the time he was twenty-eight years of age and I was twenty-one. I felt that I was in the presence of a superior being of a type to which I could not possibly attain, and I did not lose this impression throughout the spring months in which he lectured on comparative embryology at Cambridge and in which we enjoyed many long afternoons of bicycle riding on the level roads of the Fens. I always felt that Balfour *lived in a higher atmosphere, in another dimension of intellectual space. Not that he was aloof, far from it, for he was always in closest and most generous touch with the minds of his students; he made you feel that your opinion and observation were of value, although you knew all the while that your mind was still embryonic and your opinions of the most tentative order.*

Haddon had better opportunities for getting to know Balfour than had Osborne on his short visit. He attended all his lectures and Balfour described him as 'one of the best pupils I ever had'. He appointed him his Demonstrator, and letters and notes from one to the other show the intimacy between the teacher and the taught that is one of the most valuable traditions of Cambridge. A. C. H. handed on the torch and Osborne's words about Balfour (italicised above) apply with equal accuracy to his favourite pupil.[2]

[1] *Impressions of Great Naturalists,* 1924, pp. xi–xii.
[2] It was a great grief when Balfour lost his life in the Alps a few years later (1882). Haddon dedicated his first book, *Introduction to the Study of Embryology* (1887), to his 'beloved master and friend', and towards the end of his life acknowledged him as one 'to whom I owe more than I can express'.

Haddon's devotion to Balfour, 'a younger Huxley' as Foster called him, brought him into intimacy with the elder Huxley, then at the height of his powers, who later on took Balfour's place as Haddon's patron and friendly adviser (cf. p. 79). Huxley's connection with Darwin and Darwin's connection with Christ's strengthened the links. The inescapable influence of Darwin and of Darwinism on a biologist at this period received an extra stimulus in November 1877, when Cambridge, considering that it was safe to follow the lead of other Universities, conferred the distinction of an Hon. LL.D. on her famous son a few years before his death. Haddon was then entering on his third year, and he took a keen and active interest in the preparations for Darwin's reception, in which Christ's College naturally had a conspicuous part. There was a dinner at the Philosophical Club that evening at which, Darwin being unable to be present, Huxley replied to the drinking of his health and 'chaffed the dons so sweetly'. More than forty-three years later, when he was giving the Huxley Memorial Lecture, Haddon drew attention to the similarity between his own experiences in 1888 and those of 'that master of scientific method and of clear exposition' in 1850. Both of them went out to Torres Straits with special interest in marine zoology: both were then and there converted to Anthropology (cf. Bibliog. 170, 1920).

'Order is heaven's first law' A. C. H. had written in his earliest attempt to interpret the mystery of life on earth (p. 26). The work of Darwin and Huxley threw new light on the problem and suggested new methods of approach. The study of origins in the lowliest forms of life, their development, their function, and their linkage in orderly sequence had henceforth a new and fascinating interest. The careful observation of minute organisms and an attempt to discover their significance in a larger whole which characterised Haddon's zoological work in Cambridge provided the technique for the later study, not only of the physical structure of Man, but of his material culture, his handiwork, his thoughts and his religious beliefs.

Haddon had little chance of any College prize in his first year, competing with Waters (already a Scholar) and Collingridge, but at the end of the second year, though Waters takes the first place with a Natural Science Scholarship of £70, Haddon comes next with £30. There was general recognition in Christ's (expressed in letters) that this was insufficient, and the following year it was increased with a jump to £70 (Waters ahead with £80 and Rose behind with £60). He did brilliantly in his Tripos, distinguishing himself in Comparative Anatomy and Zoology, which was recognised by a nomination to the University Table at Dr Dohrn's Zoological station at Naples.

But a favourite castle in the air had to be abandoned first. It was one of the ambitions of his life to visit Ceylon where there were grand opportunities for collection and research. His relations at Colombo offered hospitality and introductions and had already established links with other residents, one of whom had arranged to provide a native collector in return for shells as his share of the booty. But he was baulked in this, as in so many of his schemes throughout his life, by lack of funds. The continuance of an allowance from home would be necessary and, as a candid aunt feels it her duty to point out, he has been a great expense to his family for some time, his father is looking much older in consequence, 'You are the eldest son and must look full in the face life's real responsibilities'.

So the tempting offer had to be given up.

There was another great disappointment this year. He applied for an Assistantship in the Zoological Department at the British Museum (under Günther), and though the commencing salary was only £150 there were chances of preferment. It was a surprise as well as a bitter disappointment when he failed in the qualifying examination. However, there was rejoicing in Cambridge. After commenting on the idiocy of examinations Professor Newton wrote: 'I look forward to your being a ministering angel in the celestial halls of Science while B. and R. [the successful candidates] lie howling under the scourges of the British Museum and other imps of the infernal regions.' Newton advised his application for the Zoological Table at Naples, and promised him work in Cambridge on his return. So with the help of special grants made by the Senate for research, A. C. H. was able to accept the nomination and to spend six months in Naples (January to June 1879) without calling on his mother for the £50 which she had offered, but which he knew could ill be spared. Here he worked with his usual vigour and industry, which were not unrewarded,[1] de-

[1] A characteristic letter from Adam Sedgwick, then Reader in Animal Morphology, later Professor of Zoology, enclosing a list of specimens wanted for Cambridge, ends with: 'and God

voting himself mainly to embryological problems and laying the foundations for the future.

His boyish hobbies with aquarium, insectarium and microscope had first interested him in lowly forms of life; Cambridge, with Balfour's search for origins, widened and deepened these interests; Naples with its opportunities for original research gave the final impetus, and for the next decade Haddon devoted himself to marine biology.

He returned to Cambridge in June 1879 and Newton appointed him Curator of the Zoological Museum and, a few months later, Demonstrator in the Department. His time was fully occupied with lectures, classes and coachings, working up the material that he had brought back from Naples, and publishing notes on special collections. He flung himself into the work of the Museum with his usual enthusiasm, rearranging, determining and exhibiting the Invertebrata, dissecting, preserving, and mounting the exhibits and illustrating them with his fine drawings. He had been warned before taking on this work that he would find his chief difficult to get on with, and so he was especially gratified with his testimonial 'I have found Haddon an agreeable colleague'.

This was a time of collecting testimonials to support applications for the very few posts then established that would give him independence and means to support a wife. For by this time Fanny Rose had taken that supreme

bless you, especially concerning the worms. I congratulate you on your epiblast discovery—that is a score. There is no news, Balfour is working like the devil. I am awful lazy.'

position in which, however many 'petticoats' there were around him, she was to reign uncontested for the rest of her life. Their engagement was announced, as has been described above (p. 47), and his appointment, through the influence of Huxley, to the Chair of Zoology in the Royal College of Science, Dublin, in December 1880, paved the way to their marriage, on September 21, 1881.

Before leaving Cambridge the mainspring of his work there may be noted. His Report to the Museums and Lecture Rooms Syndicate, 1879, makes his purpose clear: 'My great aim has been throughout to enable students to verify, as far as possible, all the statements made in their usual textbooks', and like all good teachers, he induced his pupils to teach themselves by their own observation. Even in these early days he had a wonderful power of influencing and inspiring his students, making them work and imparting enthusiasm. 'Without undue boasting I can and have done this', he writes to an intimate friend. Then, apologising for being egotistical, he supports his statement with the following anecdote:

C. first coached with Sedgwick but being so casual and inattentive S. turned him away with the characteristic remark 'I might just as well talk to a bloody post as to you' and advised him to come to me. This he did and I worked hard with him and talked to him like a father and besought him by all that he held sacred to work. He had a little money and was several times on the point of chucking up the Tripos altogether. He joined my class at Torquay in his last Long, and for his last term, to keep him at it, I coached him for nothing. Before the Tripos he admitted that if he took a first class it would be entirely owing to me. As you know he took his first. I don't say it was my *teaching*—he might have got as good elsewhere, but I certainly what the Americans call 'enthused'[1] him, which no one else did.

A long, long string of his students, including names well known throughout the world, are living proofs of this infectious enthusiasm.

---

[1] A. C. H. liked to point out the connection between enthusiasm, inspiration and insanity. 'You must be a little mad to get anywhere. You can't advance without overbalancing.'

Chapter III

DUBLIN. 1880–1900

PROFESSOR NEWTON, writing from Cambridge to his former Demonstrator and Museum Curator, congratulates him on having found promising soil in Dublin in which to work, but warns him not to take root too soon. 'When Cirripeds do so they are apt to lose their eyes and all sorts of other things—which should be an ensample unto you.' There seemed plenty of scope in Dublin for a man of energy. To the Professorship was added the post of Assistant Naturalist to the Science and Art Museum, for the management and reconstruction of which Haddon's Cambridge experiences had peculiarly qualified him, not only because his predecessor was 'a man of disorderly principles' (in a metaphorical not a moral sense as Newton is careful to point out), but also because of 'ability to get on with all and sundry. A.G.M. [his new chief] is as short of temper as of stature. This ought not to affect you. You have put up with J.W.'s rage as well as mine and are capable of weathering many storms.' This warning was unnecessary, as A.G.M. was beloved by all, but there were still many storms to be weathered both outside and inside the University. This was the distressful time of Land League disturbances, boycottings, Phoenix Park murders, police strikes and all the accompanying troubles of Home Rule agitation. Political fever ran dangerously high. Mrs Haddon's weekly letters to her mother reflect some of the violent anti-British feeling, though she tends to make light of it.

Things in Ireland are not very comfortable just now, but we are in no individual danger. Don't feel anxious about us, we are perfectly free from personal anxieties, we are only worried for poor Ireland. I really can't see which way to look for hope. . . . You have no idea what it means to be an alien in race and religion here. Even I am only just beginning to realise the intense scorn and hatred of the Irish towards all 'foreigners'.

She tells her mother of some of the 'tussles' she has had with lecturers or their wives. Once she 'let out at Mr H.' who was anticipating 'civil war', telling him it would not be 'civil war' but 'rebellion' against English law. 'That made him very angry.' But Mrs Haddon persisted:

If Home Rule is passed by Parliament and the Orangemen take up arms against the decree they are most certainly *rebels*. After that I persistently talked 'babies' to his wife and asked to see the new arrival—and we parted civilly. Alfred was tremendously amused when I told him [February 28, 1886].

One or two incidents reported in the letters may be quoted as illustrating the temper of the times. The first concerns the Royal College of Science and the reaction of the students to the news of the fall of Khartoum and the fate of Gordon:

Alfred has heard *satisfaction* expressed at the disaster and when the news came to the College of Surgeons Dr Fraser said he heard the students *cheer*. The Irish *do* hate us. . . . There have been very vicious attacks on the College [of Science] in the papers. The Lord Lieutenant came to see for himself what sort of work they are really doing. He went over the whole place thoroughly, asked searching pertinent questions and finally expressed great satisfaction with it. He was especially surprised to find that Alfred has 2 Trinity men as students [by their special request] and referred twice to it. These repeated attacks are most trying to the Professors and during the time they last Alfred gets thoroughly disheartened. If it were only *criticism* of course it would not matter, but it is nasty cavilling against the whole institution, and it plainly appears that they want the place either abolished or turned over to the Nationalists who would simply ruin it as a teaching College.

Later in the same year (1885) an elaborate programme was arranged for the visit of the Prince and Princess of Wales to Dublin, with *levées*, *soirées* and *conversaziones*; the Prince was to lay the foundation stone of the New Museum, the Princess was to receive an Honorary Degree. Dublin was all swept and garnished.

The whole city is redolent of paint and varnish, every 2nd house seems to be just painted or being done; the streets looked busier than I have ever seen them except at Xmas time.... Trinity College students have stolen the Lord Mayor's flag, which he said he would haul down when the Prince came. The students say they will fly it from Trinity and if they do there will be a row...it may lead to a serious riot as it is a political question....It would serve the Nationalists right if the Prince took them at their word and did not come. I am so disgusted with all this quarrelling that I don't feel any interest in what is coming.

But in the end all passed off well and Dublin received its royal visitors with characteristic exuberance. There was a domestic discussion as to whether A.C.H. should be presented, as some other Professors were, but the price for the court dress, etc., was prohibitive (£8. 10s. 0d.). They decided to go to the *soirée* at the College and Mrs Haddon got her old cream dress ready. She redraped the skirt, added a real lace collarette, borrowed from her mother, and with a bunch of brilliant flame-coloured nasturtiums and tiny ivy leaves 'it came out charmingly'. She was thankful that she had not launched out into a new dress as the crush was 'awful'. There was a long wait before the doors were opened, then a mad rush up into the gallery to get good seats. The staircase was littered with bits of dresses, flowers, feathers, umbrellas and other wreckage. But they got good seats in the second row and saw everything splendidly.

Royalty went to the Agricultural Show at Balls Bridge. Viceroyalty went to the Zoo. And A.C.H., a favourite alike with keepers and their charges, had to show them round. His usual Sunday treat was to get on friendly terms with all the animals, feeding the crocodiles (with raw meat on the end of a stick), 'shaking hands' with elephants, visiting the baby lions (then a rarity) and teaching the monkeys to say 'Thank you'.[1]

The elephant was brought up for the little Aberdeens to ride on. Alfred gave them biscuits for the elephant, and Ernest [then aged 4½] catching sight, rushed to him, shouting 'Father'. Lady Aberdeen said 'Would you like to ride too, darling?' and took hold of his hand to help him up, but Ernest turned shy and ran to me. Lady Aberdeen was rather nervous

---

[1] The writer remembers the joyous welcome given by the chimpanzees to A.C.H. when revisiting them in 1908 and the horny-handedness of their hearty handshake, on being properly introduced to her.

about her little ones riding alone, so one of the aide-de-camps mounted to take care of them. He looked so odd! One of the monkeys salaams for sugar and when Alfred gave the little girl some for it and said 'Salaam' the wretched thing grabbed at the child's face and very nearly scratched her. Alfred was so vexed and of course had to apologise. The monkey had before done it capitally for Ernest when no one else was there.

Politics and prejudice were constantly obstructing and embittering work in Ireland and their influence dominated University appointments. There were high hopes of a Fellowship in 1885, which would enable A. C. H. to give up the Museum work which was taking far too much of his time. 'One Catholic and one Protestant will be elected', and though Mrs Haddon pretends that she does not fix her hopes on it, she evidently lets her imagination dwell on the happy prospect.

Alfred will at once throw up the Museum post, as the Government makes up the Fellowship income to £400. Imagine Alfred among that august assembly in red and pink gowns you saw meeting to confer degrees! He will add F.R.U.I. to his other tail-end initials! Of course we are tremendously anxious for it, for it will better his position very much here, he will get larger classes at the College as he will be Examiner for the Royal University.[1]

But it was not to be, and Mrs Haddon consoles herself:

one does not feel so tied to the place as one would have been. . . . It was the National, Catholic and presumably patriotic element that combined against Alfred. All the very few scientific men on the Council were in his favour some very strongly. It's a funny place.

[1] Without this stimulus his College classes doubled in numbers, and he was obliged to give up the Museum the following year.

It was still 'funnier' when the secretary carefully explained to A.C.H. that it was not a question of merit: *'That did not even enter into the discussion.'*

In spite of all these discouragements and the unsatisfactory environment A.C.H. was putting all his energy into his work and adding not a little to his wife's anxieties.

His College work is in full swing. Mon. Tues. Wed. he has morning and evening classes, and demonstrations in the afternoons. Thurs. and Fri., classes only. On Sat. he breakfasts at the Zoo and spends his morning there and at the Museum. So 3 days a week he leaves home at 9.30 a.m. and gets back at 10.15 p.m.

Though, as was ever his wont, giving many more hours than were due both to his Department and to the Museum, he yet found time for courses of extra-University lectures, for publishing papers in scientific journals and for the more ambitious work which had been planned in Cambridge days, an introductory text-book in embryology for students (cf. Bibliog. 16). No wonder Mrs Haddon was fearful of overwork.

Professor S. is knocked up, having been working lately up to 1 at night. Alfred has been quoting him as an example of industry, now *I* quote him as a warning.

She was able to help considerably in lightening his labours, spending many hours writing letters for him (e.g. twenty copies of letters to African missionaries in districts where mud-fish might be collected, with full descriptions and directions for capture and preservation). She lured him from his work to play with the children[1] and was always planning recreations for him, inviting friends to take him out on excursions to Dalkey, Killiney, the Vale of Avoca or the Sugarloaf, and happy days were spent with the Dublin Field Club, which he and others founded in 1885.

The Haddons were not living in Dublin itself, but out at Kingstown (4 Willow Bank), and the small house with the lively children and a succession of unsatisfactory servants seems to have had its spare room always full, either of relatives for long visits or of friends for weekends throughout the year.

Dr Lloyd Praeger has supplied a description of Haddon in the Dublin period:

He was a vigorous, restless, boisterous person, impatient, full of laughter, with a rapid, rather stuttering speech, the result of his impatience. His hair was jet black, worn long, with a large lock dangling over his sallow face, and he walked rapidly with an untidy gait and a slight stoop. If you met him in the street he would probably be dressed in an old velveteen jacket, trousers baggy at the knees and fringed at the bottom, and an old hat stuck on anyhow, and he would be posting along at about four and a half miles an hour. He rather liked shocking prudish people—who according to modern standards, abounded in those days—and those whom he thought insincere or silly often thought him rude. People who knew him slightly found him an uncomfortable person but all who knew him well, loved him, he was so loyal and sincere. There were a good many people he just couldn't be bothered with, and I fancy he let them know it pretty plainly, but I don't think he had any enemies.

---

[1] The flying game was a popular one. 'The children jump from the table into Alfred's arms. They call it "flying". He calls it "exercise of faith".'

Haddon was one of the group of distinguished scientific men who used to lunch together every day at the marble-topped tables which they had presented to the Misses Gardiner's 'modest bun-shop' in Lincoln Place. Here they drank tea and ate vast quantities of hot buttered toast and discussed every subject within the confines of the universe or outside. Praeger, himself one of the party, tells of the delight and exhilaration of the lively lunch table and its brilliant company, among whom Haddon was a boisterous talker and humorous debater, conspicuous for his tremendous vitality, energy and good humour.[1]

He relates an incident which happened at Belfast characteristic of the man and his work. He was giving a University Extension course there on Zoology, and the rabbit which he had ordered had not turned up, so he asked Praeger to scour the town for one. This he did, but after a good deal of hunting he was only able to procure a large white one—alive. Haddon chloroformed it on the spot and proceeded to dissect it, hot and reeking, under the noses of his class; about a third of them never turned up again.

A member of this Belfast class describes her first encounter with Haddon. His pupils wrote papers for him and one week they were asked to describe a lugworm. She knew nothing about lugworms, save that they were used for bait, so she went to one of the Holywood fishermen and got him to dig one up for her; then she described and drew it. Haddon used to lay out the corrected papers on a table for the students to retrieve and when she reached out for hers, he stopped her and asked her to wait

[1] R. Lloyd Praeger, *A Populous Solitude*, 1941, p. 195.

63

behind after the lecture. 'And before I knew where I was, he had arranged with my father for me to go to Dublin and work with him. That was his way. He carried people with him.' This boyish impetuosity was characteristic of A. C. H. all his life long; he possessed an inexhaustible fund of energy, which was always ready to bubble up and over, sweeping waverers and objectors irresistibly along with him.

His vacations were no less strenuous than the sessions, especially when spent in dredging expeditions, which he organised and enjoyed with his usual thoroughness. He had had some experience of this combination of work and play in his Cambridge days, when he took parties of his students down to Torquay in Long Vacations, shore-collecting and going out with the trawlers and examining their hauls. Dublin Bay afforded better sport, and to this line of research he devoted many of his holidays. He soon made friends with the trawlers—he lectured to them on the habits of fishes and in return they told him of the habits not only of fishes but of fishermen, and much of his store of folklore was learnt round the coasts. It was as a trawler rather than as a Professor that he organised and led the more ambitious expeditions to the south-west coasts of Ireland, planned by Perceval Wright, Professor of Botany.

The Dredging Expedition on the *Lord Bandon*, a paddle steamer of about 150 tons, which set out from Queenstown on August 3, 1885, was the first deep-sea investigation of its kind ever attempted in Ireland, the Royal Dublin Society giving its blessing, the Royal Irish Academy and Government supplying funds.

The party included Joseph Wright (for the Foramini-
fera), W. Swanston (for the Mollusca) and S. M. Mal-
colmson (Ostracoda and Copepoda), all sturdy workers
of the Belfast Field Club; H. W. Jacob, a Dublin pupil,
undertook the higher Crustacea 'while Professor Haddon
will work up most of the remaining groups [the characteristic modesty of this quotation from a newspaper betrays
its authorship]. All practical details of the Expedition
were left to the enthusiastic co-operation of the Rev.
W. S. Green[1] of Carrigaline, Co. Cork, ably seconded by
J. E. Weeks[2] and W. H. Perrott, B.A., of Monkstown,
whose services can scarcely be overestimated'.

The official account with the scientific results was
published by the Royal Irish Academy (Bibliog. 15), but
more intimate details are to be found in letters home.

On August 5, 1885, the *Lord Bandon* steamed away
from Cork on a lovely evening, but they woke up next
morning in a rough sea, with a strong northerly wind,
and had 'an awful day', pitching, tossing and rolling, the
little boat riding over the waves like a cork. They
dredged west of Cape Clear, 'but owing to the temporary
disablement of the scientific staff the day's work was not
as satisfactory as could be wished', and even A. C. H.
confessed to being very bad all day though he was the only
one who stuck to work and he did the pickling.

Green and his friends worked splendidly all day and made
several hauls with the dredge. We got several Echinoderms

---

[1] Later Inspector of Fisheries, and just the type of adventurer
Haddon loved.
[2] Chairman of Queenstown Towing Co. which provided the
steamer.

I had never seen before. There was one Anemone which I feel certain is new to Britain and may be new to science. I have already made a coloured drawing of it.[1]

They put into quiet water in Dursey Sound, made a few hauls, had a good dinner about 5 o'clock, supper and a good night. The next day was spent in dredging across the mouth of the Kenmare River and into Ballinskellig Bay. By this time some of the party 'funked it' and were duly landed that evening. Haddon comments, 'I am not sorry T. is going as he is very cocky and appropriates specimens as if it were a game of grab'.

More settled quarters were established at Bantry where a stable provided room for sorting and pickling, but on the whole Bantry Bay did not come up to Haddon's expectations; the coast was not very good for dredging, 'I must confess to being disappointed in the beasts'. There was an excursion to a cave glowingly described in Gosse's book on sea anemones, but it was found '*very bare* of life and unsatisfactory.... Still we had a glorious time of it. We were out for 7 hours and exploded another Bantry Bay fallacy. I still swear by Dublin Bay...taking it all in all it is just about as good.'

The following summer there were some new recruits. Besides Green and Perrott in charge of navigation and sounding, and Joseph Wright and Jacob of the previous expedition, A. R. Nichols, B.A.M.R.I.A., took the place of Swanston (for the Mollusca); T. H. Thomas was included as artist; and C. B. Ball, M.D., F.R.C.S.I., was

---

[1] Of the 143 species and varieties collected sixteen were new to Britain, and showed an interesting overlapping of Lusitanian and Boreal regions off this western coast of Ireland.

PLATE II

Dredging Expedition on the *Lord Bandon*

A.C.H. (in fisherman's cap and jersey) with HAUGHTON,
GREEN (with the dredge) and C. BALL seated to the R.
R. and V. BALL standing behind.

in charge of the fishing operations, the examination of
the fish for parasites and fish evisceration. His practical
experience was valuable and luckily his services as a
doctor were not required. It will be noted on Pl. II that
his brothers Robert, Astronomer Royal of Ireland (in a
yachting cap), and Valentine, Professor of Geology at
Trinity College, are among the group assembled to give
the *Lord Bandon* a good send-off.

Again rough weather and heavy seas interfered with
the dredging and often spoilt the results, though some
new treasures were collected, notably *Edwardsia tecta*
(cf. Bibliog. 20, p. 32) and the pink anemone *Paraphellia
greenii*, named after W. S. Green. On one occasion,
south of Dursey Head, two or three of the party (including of course A. C. H.) were up at 2.30 a.m. and
lowered the dredge down to 1100 fathoms. Even with the
improvised help of the donkey engine it took three hours
to haul it up again—empty. A poor reward for seven
hours' hard labour on an empty stomach.[1]

A more careful log was kept on board S.S. *Fingal* in
1890, and although this was after Haddon's first visit to
Torres Straits, described in the next chapter, the narrative
will be added here.[2] On this trip the indispensable
Mr Green was again in charge and the party included

[1] R. Lloyd Praeger gives a lively account of his experiences on
one of these dredging expeditions instigated by Haddon and
led by Green, in 1888. He tells of the marvellous treasures of
the deep-sea trawl, of successive gales and dense fog, narrow
escapes and Green's imperturbability; 'He bore any hardship
with a laugh and no emergency disturbed his good humour'
(*The Way that I Went*, 1937. pp. 342 ff.).

[2] For sequence-dating cf. pp. xi–xii.

several colleagues and fellow-workers (E. W. L. Holt, J. E. Duerden, A. F. Dixon),[1] besides a number of Government officials. The special interest of this voyage was that investigations were to be made on behalf of the Fisheries Board to see what could be done to improve the local fishing and the condition of the natives, and A. C. H. was as much interested in the philanthropic as in the biological research. His journal notes:

The sea in this part of the world is particularly rough, the wind is nearly always blowing and that from the westerly, so that there is no real shelter on the coast line as a whole, although some bays are snug enough. The weather seems to be chronically bad—the 'wild Nor-west' as our mate is so fond of calling it is not an ideal place to live in, either on land or sea. Practical experience of this coast is considerably modifying my judgment of the natives. If I lived here I'd see the fish *blowed* before I went fishing for them in the open water—sheltered bays are right enough. But having got the fish what are they to do with them. A 20–40 miles cartage does not improve fish and it very certainly diminishes very considerably from what profit might accrue. After having reached the nearest station they have to go by train to some big town, all of which adds to the expense. Then there are so many days when the sea is too rough to fish. So the people are driven to be as much cultivators as fishermen, not that the cultivation is up to much. The country consists of

[1] E. W. L. Holt, marine biologist in the Department of Fisheries, succeeded W. S. Green as Inspector in 1915. J. E. Duerden, afterwards Curator of the Museum, Institute of Jamaica. A. F. Dixon, afterwards Professor of Anatomy, University College, Cardiff. He and his brother G.Y. collected in Dublin Bay and the latter collaborated with Haddon (cf. Bibliog. 10). *Actinoides Dixoniana* commemorates the name of both brothers (Bibliog. 44, p. 126, and 69, p. 424).

bare mountain sides and peat bogs, trees only grow in a few sheltered spots. What blame to the people if they stick to the 'stand-by' of their crops unsatisfactory though it may be. I am beginning to be hopeless about improving the fisheries of this particular district to any great extent; a good deal can be done in other places however by introducing improved methods of fishing and finding out new fishing grounds in fairly sheltered spots.

On Achill Island he had his first introduction to potheen:

We met the parish priest... he had shaved, put on his best black coat and hat and carried a book of devotion in his hand, but we did not believe that this was his normal method of going about. We went to his rooms at the Post Office and he gave us some potheen, the first I had ever tasted. When asked if he had any he said that 'by accident' he did happen to have a drop in the house. Then he apologised for what was in the decanter not being quite clear by saying he had just emptied it from the gallon jar which was standing by.... It is rather amusing to find nearly everyone with some in the house when not only the making of it but the possession of it is illegal. Everyone knows where and by whom it is made but the difficulty is to catch the maker in the act; the possession no one seems to mind. Still very little is made on the mainland as the excise officers are alert and can easily get at the people, but in the islands it is different and whenever the sea is rough and the weather sets in bad then on many an island the still is set to work, for the inhabitants know full well that it is impossible for anyone to come out to them. As soon as the weather shows signs of mending the stills are hidden and the potheen also. So the game goes on.

In the deep water off Achill Sound they shot the trawl in 220 fathoms and got a splendid haul:

Nearly 300 specimens of a long spined sea urchin, *Cidaris*, over 30 pink sea-cucumbers, the largest being 12 inches in length, 6 specimens of a large sea urchin which has a flexible shell (the 2nd or 3rd time these have been obtained in the British Isles), 6 specimens of the fine large shell *Cassidaria* which we first found in British waters during the 2nd cruise of the *Lord Bandon* several years ago, and one small octopus, besides other beasts of interest which we duly pickled for future examination.

In the deeper water off Blacksod Bay at 500 fathoms it took over an hour for the donkey engine to wind up the trawl, with a broken beam, a torn net, and a block of sandstone weighing 280 lb.:

The mate was terribly distressed at the tearing of the nets, and still more so at the wanton ripping of them to save some rare form from being smashed, for he took a professional pride in his nets; further he had to mend them when they were torn or cut. As no one had ever dredged off this coast at this particular depth we were quite content to have the beasts even at the expense of a torn trawl and broken beam. We got some good things.

More exciting things were collected on land.

The Allies who owned the island of Inishbofin were interested in antiquities and folklore and told Haddon of a derelict church containing some skulls. This aroused his head-hunting passion and he determined to secure some— the first to be collected in this part of the world. With the connivance of the Allies he and his Dublin pupil, Dixon, arranged a plan of action. All were going ashore that night and when it was dark the two conspirators were shown the way to the churchyard.

We two climbed over the gate, went down the enclosure which is practically a large graveyard, disturbing some cattle, stumbled along and entered the church, tumbling over the grave stones. In the corner we saw by the dim light the skulls in a recess in the wall. There must have been 40 or more, all broken, mostly useless, but we found a dozen which were worth carrying away, only one however having the face bones. Whilst we were thus engaged we heard 2 men slowly walking along the road and like Brer Fox we lay low and like the Tar Baby, 'kept on saying nothing'. When the coast was clear we put our spoils in the sack and cautiously made our way back to the road. Then it did not matter who saw us. The sailors wanted to take the sack when we got back to the boat but Dixon would not give it up and when asked what was in it said 'Potheen'. So without any further trouble we got the skulls aboard and then we packed them in Dixon's portmanteau and locked it and no one except our two selves had any idea that there are a dozen human skulls on board and they shan't know either (cf. Bibliog, 54).

Most of the time was devoted to marine research, but human problems grew more and more insistent and intrusive. In Connemara Haddon met Miss Southern, acting superintendent of the Connemara Industries, and went over the knitting school and heard of the work that various ladies were doing to start and market local products. Miss Southern had settled in this remote spot

to identify herself with the people, in fact constituting herself a kind of economic lay missionary. This is the sort of thing that appeals to my sympathy far more than proselytising,

and he showed his sympathy in practical form by buying some locally hand-knitted socks. Later they had a visit from the ladies and Father Flannery, and he notes with a spice of malice the result of having women and priests on board.

The combination is fatal, and it was not to be wondered at that we had bad luck; we not only caught no fish worth having but we got hitched and broke the beam of the trawl and tore the nets.

This had however happened when neither women nor priests were on board (cf. p. 70).

There was a further invasion of these fatal visitors on the Sunday, for Father Flannery had given out from the altar that everyone should pay a visit to the *Fingal* 'as we had come to help them develop the fisheries and to teach them how to fish better'. So men, women, boys and girls all came out in their boats, together with three priests, and after they had seen all the sights with exclamations of 'Glory be to God' the entertainment ended with the weighing of the priests in the scales with wild speculations and much merriment.

That evening there was a party at Father Flannery's house.

We had a great time, most of the conversation turning on the fishing. It is impossible to give a description of the whole affair. I enjoyed it immensely as it was a peep into another world and many of the ways of thought and ways of looking at things were very different from what I have been accustomed to. It is becoming more and more evident to me that the ordinary Saxon is incapable of understanding the typical Irish. How much less is he capable of governing him! Cut-and-dried rules and methods of procedure are useless. Theory is all very fine; the facts of Irish idiosyncrasies refuse to be treated in a logical manner and they are stubborn facts too.

On a similar expedition the following year on S.S. *Harlequin*, Connemara was visited again. Here Haddon met Miss Alice Balfour and Lady Zetland, wife of the Viceroy, who were travelling round the congested districts to see conditions for themselves. Father Flannery invited the Viceregal party to a luncheon:

I was delighted to sit next Miss Balfour and made the most of my opportunity as I have long been anxious to meet her for various reasons. She is wonderfully pleasant—not good-looking, but very intelligent looking, with honest kindly eyes, and a very pleasant smile is constantly playing on her face. I began talking about Frank Balfour—his influence and his work in Cambridge—about mutual friends—and so on and we immediately were *en rapport* with each other and talked straight. It is a peculiarity of Miss B. which she shares with her brother the Chief Secretary to go straight to the heart of the matter without beating about the bush. This is just what my soul likes —so we dispensed with all small talk and generalities and started and continued on fundamentals. It was one of the most refreshing talks I have had for a long time. I told her about my new method of studying art from a biological standpoint[1] in which she expressed herself much interested. Having a good knowledge of the general principles of Biology we could get over the ground quickly and I had not to explain my drift or elaborate details thereof. Later in the day I had other chats with her, when we spoke about the Fisheries. It appears that she is getting up this subject for her brother. He has no time to make himself master of all the details of every subject connected with Irish industries so she is relieving him of this and is learning all she can in order to digest it for him. I am particularly glad of this as this gave me an opportunity for 'cutting in' and I much hope that when they return to Dublin in the autumn I shall have a further opportunity of helping to put

[1] As seen in *Decorative Art of New Guinea*, 1894, and *Evolution in Art*, 1895.

the fisheries on a more scientific basis than has hitherto been the case. If I can assist in this I shall feel that my time in Ireland has not been misspent, nor the years that I have devoted to Marine Zoology of Ireland misapplied. I trust this will give me the chance of doing Holt[1] a good turn at the same time. Personally I do not expect to reap any benefit from what I hope will be a new departure but one can't be always bothered with looking after personal interests and others want helping far more than I do.[2]

There was a sumptuous luncheon and after the sweets Lady Zetland drank some potheen.

It was very characteristic of the topsy-turvy spirit of this country to see Her Majesty's representative drinking illicit liquor and thereby countenancing illegality.

Later on Lady Zetland and Miss Balfour visited S.S. *Harlequin* to see the scientific work on board and the latter was especially interested in the fish–eggs and embryos as she had drawn such things for her brother Frank many years before. She could hardly tear herself away and even kept the representative of Royalty waiting.

[1] Cf. footnote, p. 68.
[2] His work for the Fisheries was successful and appreciated. Grenville Cole, Professor of Geology at the Royal College of Science, wrote (Feb. 3, 1915) to tell Haddon of the farewell dinner given to W. S. Green who was vacating the Presidency of the Fisheries Board in favour of Holt. He says: "Tacitus... describes a procession in Imperial times in which the statues of Brutus and Cassius were *not* carried; and thereby they were more remembered than if they had been present. This was the feeling of so many of us in regard to last night....The fishery work will go on with its scientific side well organised, but your planning of the original surveys will always be at the back of it."

Other vacations were no less strenuous, and most of them were, when possible, spent abroad, meeting fellow-workers and comparing material. There were many visits to the United States and Canada and the beginnings of many life-long friendships.[1] There were 'museum crawls' on the Continent and note-books filled with sketches. But the expenses of all these trips had to be severely restricted and frugal habits made a little go a long way. Take, for example, a day in Venice as described in a letter home.

Directly we got up we boiled some water in a kettle over a spirit lamp and made some tea which we drank with lemons as we had no milk. we had two little rolls each and some fruit which we had bought the day before. Then we went out sight-seeing. When we were hungry again in the middle of the day we usually bought some rolls at a bakers and some fruit at a fruit stall and ate it by the side of a canal, sometimes I would buy some roast chestnuts. Then we went on sightseeing till it was dark. after we had gone back to our rooms and had a wash we went out to dinner at a restaurant. After dinner (which was at 7.0 or 7.30) we went to a large square outside the Cathedral and had coffee at a café and listened to the band and watched the crowds of people walking up and down. about 9 o'c we went back to our rooms to write letters and to go to bed.[2]

One visitor to Dublin during the busy years of Haddon's Professorship there must be mentioned; this was Eugene

[1] The list of his American friends would fill a page, and it seems invidious to make a selection, but mention must be made of his particular 'home from home' with the Furness family at Wallingford, Delaware County, Pennsylvania, where he re-velled in unaccustomed luxuries.

[2] Extract from a diary in the form of letters home, mostly to the children, charmingly illustrated with coloured sketches.

Dubois, who, accompanied by what remained of *Pithecanthropus erectus*, came over at Haddon's invitation in November 1895. The first account of the discovery was the description published in Java in 1894, and though the fossils had been exhibited at the International Congress of Zoologists at Leiden in September 1895, only one or two British scientists had actually seen them. In January 1895 D. J. Cunningham, Professor of Anatomy at Trinity College, Dublin, had read a paper before the Royal Dublin Society on microcephalous idiots, and he had suggested that the new aspirant for a place in the human family tree might belong to this group. As the result of Haddon's efforts, Dubois came over to read a paper before the same society frankly entitling it 'A transition form between Man and Apes',[1] and his presentation of the problem before the British Association the following year (also at Haddon's instigation) secured the inclusion of *Pithecanthropus erectus* in the human ancestry, though his relative position is still controversial. On his return to Leiden after the Dublin visit Dubois wrote:

Still I think of your great kindness you had towards me and of the pleasure of meeting you. I even now see you running and hurrying for helping me before and after the session.

And though their ways did not meet again, he wrote nearly twenty years later (this time on the subject of the Wadjak Man):

I have never forgotten meeting you...that single occasion does occupy the foreground of the memory images of my life.

[1] Published in *Sci. Trans. R.D.S.* vol. VI, 1896.

In spite of all the activities that he succeeded in crowding into his life A. C. H. was all the time, in his own words, 'perishing for want of research', and for opportunities that Dublin could not, or would not, give him; he reluctantly owned 'the Department here is played out'; but there were few openings anywhere else. This was the age of Professorships of Natural History— 'Professors of Creation' as he called them—which included not only Zoology and Botany but also Geology and Palaeontology, these latter often tethered more or less to the Old Testament.

He applied for the new Professorship of Biology to be established in Melbourne, with twice or three times his Dublin salary, and was placed on the select list. A friend, a member of the Selection Committee, writes to tell him he will be required for an interview in London. '*For inspection*. Get your hair cut.' But all efforts were vain and A. C. H. was thrown back on his own resources. He felt more and more dissatisfied with his work, lecturing about coral reefs and tropical fauna which he had never seen. He described himself as 'retailing second-hand goods over the counter' and determined to go off to some marine biological hunting ground to make his own observation. He could remember the very day and the very spot on the cliffs of Howth when he first broached the subject to his wife and how she agreed without a murmur. He began to make his plans, discussing the more favourable areas, and his final choice narrowed down to three: (1) Ascension, (2) West Indies, (3) Torres Straits. He consulted experts and each spot had its supporter.

Moseley[1] of the *Challenger* expedition wrote enthusiastically in favour of Ascension, on account of the turtles:

What can a man possibly want better than to have numbers of gravid laying female turtles collected for him by steam launches all round the island and shut up in big pens where they must lay their eggs within reach. I cannot conceive any more favourable conditions. I have tried them myself.

A. R. Wallace advised the West Indies:

I would certainly *not* advise you to go to Torres Straits for what you want. Besides the great distance, which would cause you to spend nearly half of your year in travelling and waiting (going and returning) you would probably be subject to great trouble and delay about men, boats, etc., and many of the islands are unhealthy. It seems to me that you would get *all* you want with many incidental advantages in the West Indies. You have coral reefs and oceanic depths and grand tropical vegetation in some of the islands. You would have the great advantage there of facility in locomotion.... You would find servants and living pretty cheap and be able to make the most of your time. You would probably meet with much hospitality and be able to work in a comfortable house with civilised surroundings.

A comfortable house and civilised surroundings were of no importance to A. C. H., and a letter that came at the same time as that of Wallace tipped the scales in favour of Torres Straits. This was from the Rev. S. Macfarlane, former L.M.S. missionary in Polynesia and Melanesia, and it contained practical offers of help. Macfarlane had retired from the mission field and was living in Bedford,

[1] H. N. Moseley, Professor of Anatomy, Oxford.

so the Roses formed a friendly link. He wrote offering introductions to his successor, Mr Savage, who would act as host on Murray Island, and to the Hon. John Douglas, Resident on Thursday Island. He plans out the route and proposes that the little mission steamer should meet Haddon at Thursday Island, take him to Murray Island which he would make his headquarters. There he could get men, boats, and anything he wanted. 'Spend August to December there and in New Guinea and you need fear no evil. . . . Going as my friend I don't think you would have much trouble.'

Huxley's approval was probably the decisive factor, not only because of his knowledge of Torres Straits, gained when on the *Rattlesnake* survey, but also because of his position in the world of science and his influence in obtaining grants. For many years Haddon had been in the habit of consulting him about his work, and after Balfour's tragic death in 1882 Huxley takes the latter's place as guide, philosopher and friend. A letter from Huxley in October 1882 offers help in the sorting out of the *Challenger* Lamellibranchs and continues:

No one will make good Balfour's loss—he was the man of the future—but if a man of the past is any good, I shall always be glad to be at your service in the way of counsel.

His counsel with regard to Torres Straits was favourable:

I know Darnley Island hard by your proposed quarters and I should think the locality very good for your purpose. . . . It is as hot as need be, and oppressively so in the rainy season, but there was no sickness among us the whole time.

He adds:

I will willingly support your application for a grant and I hope there will be no difficulty about it. I am sure to be up [in London] for a day or two and if you will come and dine with me some evening we can talk the whole business over.

The application was for a grant of £300 and Haddon's roughly scribbled first draft of the scheme was as follows:

I propose to investigate the fauna, structure and mode of formation of the coral reefs in Torres Straits, more especially at the Murray Islands,...to map the raised and submerged coral formations,...to determine the angle of the slope of the reefs in various directions...to investigate the fauna of the lagoons of the shore exposed at low tide and of the submarine slope (if possible down to 100 fathoms), to endeavour to determine the zones of different species of coral and of associated invertebrates, and also what conditions of light, temperature and currents are favourable or otherwise for the different species. With the information thus obtained to study the raised coral formation on various islands and on New Guinea so as to be able to approximately determine the exact conditions under which the various formations were found.

This was the programme A. C. H. set before him for which he obtained a grant of £300; what he accomplished with it was something very different.

Chapter IV

TORRES STRAITS AND NEW GUINEA
1888–1914

1. 1888–1889

In his *History of Anthropology* (1910, p. 3) Haddon
divides anthropologists into two classes, field-workers
and arm-chair workers, the former collecting the data
which the latter 'weld into coherent hypotheses'. He
adds 'the most valuable generalisations are made, however, when the observer is at the same time a generaliser'.
This dualism was the secret of his success, for he was a
rapid, indefatigable and scrupulously accurate observer,
yet few field-workers have taken such world-wide views
or been so daring in their general deductions (cf. especially
Races of Man (1909), and *Wanderings of Peoples* (1911)).

The story of his anthropological work may be divided
in a similar way, part having been spent in the field and
part in the study, and it will be more convenient if the
two lines of research are treated separately rather than
strictly chronologically.[1]

His first visit to Torres Straits in the summer of 1888
was the turning point in his life, and had a profound
influence not only on his subsequent career but on the
world of science. He went out, as was seen in the last
chapter, as a marine biologist, with a special interest in
coral reefs and their fauna. To this study he devoted his

[1] For sequence-dating cf. Table, pp. xi–xii.

working days, which, even in the enervating climate of the tropics, were seldom less than twelve hours long.[1] His carefully kept journal is full of detailed observation and delightful sketches, and room can be found here for only a few extracts, but any page taken at random will show how the interest in marine biology was gradually eclipsed by interest in the natives and more particularly in their customs, which were rapidly being abandoned and forgotten. So the long days collecting on the reef, exploring in the bush, sorting and preserving in the improvised laboratory or writing in his hut, were followed by evenings surrounded by natives 'yarning', and, as he gained their confidence, relating what happened 'before white man he come'. These human contacts were not altogether unplanned. He had always intended to make the most of his opportunities of seeing and learning what he could of his first 'savages';[2] he had also a secondary motive for getting in touch with them as he hoped to recoup himself for some of the expenses of his journey by collecting 'curios' for museums.

He left Tilbury in July 1888 on the S.S. *Taroba*, and his journal records his first impressions of the island world with which his name will always be associated.

[1] Seligman used jokingly to complain that A. C. H. couldn't trust the sun to get up unless he was there to see that it started work punctually.

[2] 'Savage' is here used in the Haddonian sense. He was careful to define it both as noun and as adjective. Noun means 'dweller in the woods, i.e. backward people driven into out-of-the-way places'. Adjective means 'containing all those bad qualities which have been produced by contact with stronger peoples'.

On Aug. 8 we could make out the advance guard of Australia...soon we sighted Prince of Wales Island...and in due course we reached my Promised Land...Thursday Island. It was not long before I discovered that I had indeed fallen on my feet, comfortably housed and kindly entertained by the boss of this part of the world, Mr H. Milman.[1] Not only have I for the present free quarters and all comfort, but I can accompany Mr Milman in all his official rounds and when not otherwise engaged I may have free use of the Government steam launch. My good fortune is thus far ahead of my most sanguine anticipations.

He had unexpected good fortune with 'curio' collecting too, and especially in his head-hunting. He had heard of the decorated skulls obtained from Nagir, and on visiting the island with Mr Milman on August 13, he made inquiries of a man in pidgin English and drew a sketch to show what he wanted.

He savvied quickly and went off, soon returning with the skull, artificial eyes, decorated face and all, in a basket, for which we bartered a trade hatchet, 3 fathoms of calico, say about 5/- prime cost to me (cf. *Head-Hunters*, p. 181, Pl. XII).

He made a rich haul of masks, tobacco pipes (the nucleus of the fine monograph which he finished just before his death; Bibliog. 220), besides ornaments sacred and profane, clubs, bows and arrows. One bundle of the latter was handed over with the caution 'No good arrows. Man he die. S'pose he shot' to explain that they were believed to be poisoned.

The conviction that in a few years anthropological

---

[1] Acting Government Resident (in the absence of the Hon. John Douglas), after whom *Thoe*, later *Sagartia milmani*, was named. Cf. Bibliog. 44, p. 130, and 69, p. 461.

investigation would be too late was illustrated on Yam (Turtlebacked Island):

We found near the landing-stage a wind-screen or break-wind under which a few men were squatting. The total inhabitants of the island had dwindled down to 3 men and 2 boys only. All the women were dead or had migrated to neighbouring islands. The old men were sitting still, listlessly, doing nothing, caring for nothing, and waiting to join the majority. I felt quite sad about them.

At Tut or Warrior Island Haddon first met Maino, the *mamoose* (chief), who became his devoted friend, and invaluable interpreter of ancient customs. He arranged a native dance at which he himself played the drum, but injudiciously sent a message to the women performers to tell them to put on their calico gowns, which spoilt the effect; and it took much persuasion to induce one of them to wear her grass petticoat instead.[1] At Mowatta Haddon assisted at the installation of the *mamoose*, who was invested with the staff of office (a japanned walking stick with a shilling inserted in the handle). Here also he first met with 'sister-exchange in the raw, like a case not unknown to us',[2] which he describes in a letter home. The Resident had to adjudicate in the case of an eligible youth who wanted to marry a girl but had no sister to offer in return, and the difficulty was overcome by means of a money payment, the newly ennobled chief having to sanction the innovation. It was a great disappointment here to find the women 'decently clothed in long calico gowns', but they were induced to abandon these atrocities

[1] This is described in *Head-Hunters*, pp. 174 ff.
[2] Cf. p. 46.

for their grass petticoats on the occasion of a dance 'and looked much better'.

After a preliminary tour of the islands, observing and collecting information, Mabuiag was chosen for a longer residence:

Mr Milman gave the chief instructions to do whatever I wanted. I am to have full use of the govt whaleboat and the 4 water police. I shall in fact be chief of the island and the only white man there.

Here he settled at the mission station (August 18 to October 26), established a laboratory some half mile away at a deserted pearling station and began collecting on the surrounding reefs with the help of the *mamoose* and three or four natives.

The men were very anxious to do their best and were chuckling the whole time and great was their delight when they picked up things I cared for and kept. I was fortunate enough to find some living blue coral (*Heliopora cærulea*),[1] and I believe I am one of the very few zoologists who have seen the polyps expanded. Spent the rest of the day drawing and preserving beasts,...later on several men came in to talk and I obtained some interesting information.

Another day there was an expedition into the bush, and the first encounters with wild bamboo and parasitic Formicaria; but the special collection was (to the great amusement of the natives) some slime and mud from the bottom of the pools.

I examined this and found that I might just as well have been looking at some material from a peaty moorland of the old

[1] Cf. Bibliog. 28, 1890.

country. Most if not all of the forms appeared to be of identical species with our own.

He describes a typical day on Mabuiag.

I rise about 6 o'clock and have a cup of cocoa and some bread (made by my boy) do a little writing and so on, have a dip in the sea and dress, such as it is, trowsers, flannel shirt and belt. No socks or boots save when going on a long tramp, though I carry slippers to put on when going over the rocks to my laboratory which is half a mile away. Breakfast at 8. bread, possibly eggs or fresh fish or tinned fish or anything which may be by me, rice, sometimes sweet potatoes or yams and tea. After breakfast I go collecting, either dredging or shore work, or when I need exercise for a long ramble in the bush. Low tides occur between 5 and 6 o'clock, then I have to get up at 5, get the crew up and start in 'small daylight' to some outlying reef. More than once it was only by a great effort that I could summon up sufficient energy to get off early, but I would not set a bad example to the men. After collecting for some time I return to my lab. and sort my captures, preserving most but keeping some alive. Luncheon about 1 o'clock consists sometimes of a plate of soup and always of rice and tinned fruit. I drink water and lime juice, (the water from an iron rain-water tank—it is a bit rusty but wholesome enough). After resting and reading for a few minutes in my hammock I return to the lab. and draw, observe and make notes till sunset. Then I go home, have dinner, 6 or 6.30, of tinned meat, fresh potatoes, rice and tinned fruit, rarely fish, less rarely dugong meat. A swell dinner consists of dugong soup, dugong fritters, dugong steak, potatoes, rice and peaches. After dinner I read a short time inside the house as outside the S.E. trade wind blows too strongly to keep my lamp alight. My Mabuiag 'best hundred books' consists of *Amelia, Waverley*, Emerson's *Social aims and other essays* and the *Pall Mall Budget*. The Bible is my nightcap. At 7 I join the missionary camp folk at evening prayer. Imagine a blazing wood fire beneath a grove of young coconut palms, the fitful flames throwing up their grey stems and waving feathery leaves against the encircling gloom. Around the fire the worshippers sit on their haunches on the ground; as the gusts of wind cause the flames to veer round and break into a blaze, so the light reveals the dark faces or loses them in the general darkness. All are completely clothed I am sorry to say in usually very grimy costumes, the only individuals who look well are the few young men and boys who occasionally have nothing on but their 'calico', or waistcloth. Service commences with a hymn and strangely does a familiar tune sound when wedded to native words and sung with native accent and emphasis, and original variations. A little scripture is read. Then a prayer follows. The service may be conducted by Hakin, the Lifu teacher, or by the Lifu schoolmaster or by a native Christian. The officiate squats on a mat and by his side I sit on a camp-stool. I was much amused when at the close of the service on my first evening here the conductor turned round to me and, just as if we had come out of church in England, politely remarked on the pleasantness of the weather.

I return to my house, take my daily potion of quinine and then friends drop in to have a chat, from 2 or 3 to as many as 2 dozen, and I endeavour to find out all I can about what they did 'before white man he come—no missionary—no nothing'. We have very pleasant times together, laughing and talking. They are very ready to tell me all they can but too often the reply is 'Me young man. (some 30 or so with a beard) me no savvy—old man he savvy.' Descriptions of get-up for dances etc. are elucidated by my making rough sketches of a man, then filling up in detail by degrees and great is their delight when the totality is before them. About half past nine or ten o'clock we say *Yawa*. If not too tired I do some writing, then turn in.

When he returned to Thursday Island in September
and sorted out his loot everyone was astonished at his
collections. No one had ever seen such things before,
and few knew that they even existed in the islands.

But I value the information I have gathered concerning the
things as being of more value. There is no merit in mere collecting and I have been fortunate enough to have had the benefit
of Mr Milman's knowledge and authority and to arrive at a
time when the old order is changing, giving place rather to a
negation than to a 'new'. They know, poor souls, that they
have now no need for these things, but they *have* need for baccy.
Never again will anyone have the chance I have.... I really
have had wonderful luck.

After several weeks at Mabuiag in the western Torres
Straits, he paid a long visit to Murray Island (Mer) in
the Eastern (volcanic) group, finding different types of
flora and fauna, including man. Here the missionaries
Mr Savage and Mr Hunt[1] were his hosts, but he was left
in charge of the island during their absence and had most
unexpectedly to deal with a labour strike. It was such
good hunting here that even though he prolonged his stay
to mid-April he felt that he had only skimmed the surface;
so much more remained to be done that a return visit was
imperative in the interests of anthropology rather than
marine biology. The Cambridge Anthropological Expedition to Torres Straits and New Guinea (1898–9), the
first and in many ways the model of its kind, was already

---

[1] Rev. A. E. Hunt of the London Missionary Society, after
whom *Paraphellia hunti* was named (Bibliog. 44, p. 129; 69,
p. 461).

conceived in the final pages of the journal of 1888–9, written at Murray Island.

A proper anthropologist requires wider knowledge and more versatile talents than I can lay claim to. He should be a linguist, artist, musician and have an extensive knowledge of natural and mechanical science etc....

Haddon was neither linguist nor musician, but he had the one thing needful for a field anthropologist, without which all work is barren, the gift for friendship. He was no respecter of persons, or rather he was a respecter of persons as persons, regardless, if not actually disapproving, of accidents of rank or wealth. He offered comradeship to honest workers in any walk of life and had a kindly tolerance even for the dishonest slackers, but he hated pretentiousness and superficiality. He had no society manners, and his blunt, downright outspokenness was often disconcerting in conventional circles; but with the simpler and less cultured folk there was a sympathy and understanding that overcame timidity; acquaintance and friendship seem to have been synonymous terms, and it was this 'Haddonian touch' that made the Torres Straits researches not only possible but of surpassing value.

In April the journal ends abruptly. The rest of the tour can be traced by means of occasional letters.

The work both on Mabuiag and on Murray Island was interrupted by trips to New Guinea (with the Rev. James Chalmers, or Tamate, as he preferred to be called) (cf. Bibliog. 87); to Australia, to stay with the Jardines, the pioneer cattle ranchers of the district; and on leaving the islands on his homeward way he spent some weeks in

Victoria and New South Wales. A visit to the Rev. W. W. Gill near Sydney strengthened his sense of the importance of saving vanishing data, to which the rest of his life was mainly devoted. Mr Gill could tell of the vast changes that had taken place even in the last few years. In a letter written shortly after Haddon's visit, he says:

In 1872 Thursday Island had no inhabitants save a few roaming aboriginals. I spent a night on what is now Cookstown; no sound whatever save the hum of insects and the twitterings of drowsy birds. But as 'civilisation' advances much that is of deepest interest to you and to me disappears for ever. You do well to pick up the crumbs that remain.

It had been largely the influence of Mr Gill that diverted A. C. H. from a business to a scientific career (cf. pp. 20–1). The same influence now helped to divert him from Zoology to Anthropology.

On returning home to Dublin in 1889 there was an immense amount of work to be done in sorting out his zoological results, and attention is here drawn to these items since the pre-eminence he afterwards attained in Anthropology is apt to obscure the eminence he had already attained in Zoology. His *Introduction to the Study of Embryology* which he had published in 1887, though only designed as a text-book for the use of students, was welcomed as a real addition to a little-known subject, the importance of which was gaining recognition, and a reviewer (in the *Dublin Journal of Medical Science*, (3), No. CXCI, 1887) hailed it as 'the best of the three modern English works on the subject'.[1] The book contained a

[1] How few young authors, finding this verdict on their firstborn, would pencil 'untrue' in the margin!

considerable amount of original work which he had done under Balfour's supervision at Cambridge, together with fresh discoveries from his work at Naples. Here he had devoted himself mainly to the Actiniaria, and these researches were supplemented later by his collecting expeditions round the Irish coasts.

Haddon saw that the study of the British species could advance no further until we possessed a knowledge of their anatomy on the basis of which a sound system of classification could be built up, and his introduction of the anatomical and embryological *motif* represented a distinct advance on earlier work.[1]

After his return from Torres Straits his divergent interests are clearly shown. In 1889 'Zoological Notes from Torres Straits' appeared in *Nature*, but in the same year he chose as the subject of his paper at the British Association 'Former Customs and Beliefs of the Torres Straits Islanders'; and together with the 'Reports on the Zoological Collections made in Torres Straits', published later by the Royal Dublin Society, 'Manners and Customs of the Torres Straits Islanders' appeared in *Nature* and 'Legends of Torres Straits' in *Folk Lore* (cf. Bibliog. pp. 154–5).

These papers attracted the attention of anthropologists. J. G. Frazer, who had just published his book on Totemism, wrote in July 1890:

Allow me to congratulate you on the splendid results of your stay in Torres Straits. [Your papers] form a most valuable contribution to anthropology. Indeed they are priceless, since

[1] Cf. H. J. Fleure, 'Alfred Cort Haddon', *Obituary Notices of the Royal Society*, 1940, pp. 451–2.

the information they contain, if it had not been collected by you, would probably have entirely vanished.

With characteristic generosity and modesty he adds:

Work like yours will be remembered with gratitude long after the theories of the present day (mine included) are forgotten, or remembered only to be despised as obsolete and inadequate.

He urged Haddon to publish all his material as a monograph, assuring him that many anthropologists would find it of great value.

A monograph on the ethnography of the islanders[1] was indeed already planned, but no one was more conscious than A. C. H. that the material was incomplete and that a return visit and more intensive work were essential. This however entailed two important transitions, first from Zoology to Anthropology; next, from Dublin to Cambridge; and he was doubtful of the wisdom of both. Nor was the desire overmastering, as he records.[2]

He had arranged to have a couple of months in London before returning to his duties in Dublin and spent most of the time in sorting out his ethnographical collections in the British Museum, to which most of the specimens were given, and in writing the papers for the Anthropological Institute's *Journal* and for *Folk Lore*. All this

---

[1] The volume of the *Reports* dealing with the general ethnography of Torres Straits was not in fact completed until nearly half a century later (cf. p. 145). It is characteristic of Haddon that he did not notice until too late that the title-page of this volume of some 400 pages, summarising his life work, omitted his name, which only appears on the dust cover.

[2] Introduction to vol. I of the *Reports* (1935, pp. xi–xii).

brought him for the first time into contact with ethnologists, folklorists and others interested in Anthropology. Sir William Flower,[1] recognising his ability and enthusiasm, suggested that he should seriously take up the study of Anthropology, but this he was unwilling to do as he felt wedded to Zoology.

He always insisted that he was fundamentally a zoologist, but Torres Straits had revealed the lure of Anthropology, and after his return to Dublin he strayed more and more on to the border line between the two branches of science, organising a scheme for the ethnographical survey of Ireland, and inaugurating it with papers on the Aran Islanders (Bibliog. 42). It was a reversal of the usual order of things and a new vision of anthropological research that training acquired in Torres Straits should be applied to investigation in the British Isles. Both led to the same conviction that research if done at all must be done at once. Zoology could wait. Man's life history was changing more rapidly. He determined to devote his future to the study of Man.

Before making the plunge he consulted Huxley, who wrote from Eastbourne (November 6, 1889):

I know of no department of natural science more likely to reward a man who goes into it thoroughly than anthropology. There is an immense deal to be done in the science pure and simple and it is one of those branches of inquiry which brings one into contact with the great problems of humanity in every direction. I have dabbled in it a good deal and I should have liked nothing better than to give myself up to it. It would certainly be necessary to acquaint yourself thoroughly with

[1] Director of the Natural History Museum, British Museum.

what they have been doing in Paris—and after that I should say with what is being done in Berlin—also a visit to Italy to see what wonderful materials have of late years been collected there bearing on archaic races. The only part of your project in which I am afraid to give you any encouragement is the expectation that when the labourer is thus carefully prepared —his hire will be forthcoming. I admire Mrs Haddon's and your pluck immensely, but after all you know there is an irreducible *minimum* of bread and butter the need of which is patent to a physiologist if not to a morphologist and I declare with sorrow that at this present writing I do not see any way by which a devotee of anthropology is to come at the bread—let alone the butter. And you must recollect (*experto crede*) that the necessity of having to make an income, independently of one's proper work, is a frightful burden upon anyone who desires to do that work as it ought to be done. Don't burn your ships in a hurry. I am very glad to see you men safe back—and I should like to hear of your travels among my old friends in Torres Straits. But though I am wonderfully better I am still unable to do much talking and I cannot bring you down here for a mere half-hour's chat.

' Don't burn your ships in a hurry ' referred to Haddon's suggestion that he should give up the Dublin Professorship (the Museum Assistantship with the additional income of £200 a year had been resigned owing to pressure of work in 1886) and seek his fortune in Cambridge; the caution was effective, as though the Haddon family moved to Cambridge in 1893 the post in Dublin was not relinquished, and a much too busy and uneasy life was spent between the two, until, in 1901, the belated[1] election to

---

[1] In 1882 the Master told Professor Newton that Haddon would have been made a Fellow that year had he remained in Cambridge.

a Fellowship at Christ's, supplemented by lecturing, writing and reviewing, secured 'the irreducible minimum of bread and butter'.

2. CAMBRIDGE ANTHROPOLOGICAL EXPEDITION TO TORRES STRAITS AND NEW GUINEA. 1898-1899

The great enterprise with which Haddon's name will always be associated was dreamed of in 1889, but several busy anxious years passed before the outlines of the scheme took shape, and no one save the organiser and his immediate circle could guess how much time, thought and energy were given to the planning of the Expedition, or how much faith and determination were needed to overcome all discouragements.

The first question was to find the men: it was equally necessary to find the money.

Haddon had decided that a party of six investigators should be both maximum and minimum, knowing the difficulties of housing, transport, food and the provision of apparatus, and he set about collecting his team. During the 1888–9 visit to the islands he had been conscious of his own limitations, especially in two spheres, music and languages (cf. p. 89). He could describe dances, but was deaf to the accompanying tunes; he could collect vocabularies, but they were merely lists of words. So a musician and a linguist must be of the company. Furthermore, he was convinced that a successful investigator must have a true insight into the minds of the investigated and understand their reactions and ways of thought. So a trained psychologist was essential. But psychology did not mean 'brain-spinning', for which he had a supreme contempt; like everything else it had to be firmly grounded on experiment, and his first choice fell on W. H. R. Rivers, who was at that time lecturing to the Cambridge Medical School on the physiology of the senses.

But Rivers refused and Haddon had to look elsewhere.

C. S. Myers,[1] one of Rivers's most brilliant pupils, had attended Haddon's lectures on Human Anatomy for the Natural Sciences Tripos in 1895; he was already interested in Anthropology and had published an account of the Brandon skulls collected by Macalister (*J. Anthrop. Inst.* 1895). As he was moreover an accomplished musician and played the violin, the combination was just what was wanted, and Myers was the first member of the Expedition to be appointed.

W. McDougall[2] was another of Rivers's pupils, a year senior to Myers; he had had practical work in St Thomas's Hospital, and at Myers's suggestion he

[1] Besides his pioneer work, *Textbook of Experimental Psychology* (1922), mainly the result of his field work, Myers's studies in primitive music broke new ground. (The disintegration of his violin in the tropical damp of Torres Straits was one of the few irreparable disasters of the Expedition.) After being Professor of Psychology at King's College, London, he was appointed Principal of the National Institute of Industrial Psychology. Writing to A.C.H. in 1935 he said: 'I always look on you as the prime cause of my adult career...and as the partial creator of the Institute.'

[2] Well known as a pioneer in social psychology, later Professor of Psychology at Duke University, U.S.A. It was his introduction to C. Hose (cf. p. 103) that led to their collaboration in *The Pagan Tribes of Borneo* (1912).

PLATE III

Torres Straits, 1898

A. C. HADDON seated in centre

L. to R. W. H. R. RIVERS, C. G. SELIGMAN, S. H. RAY, and A. WILKIN

The complete group was published in *Man*, 1941, **90**.

was invited to join the Expedition. To quote Haddon's report:

When Rivers found that his two best students were going he asked whether after all he might come too. Naturally I was ᵣery much pleased at this though I own that I felt that the psychological side was rather overweighted. I put the direction of the psychological department entirely into the hands of Rivers and for the first time psychological observations were made on a backward people in their own country by trained psychologists with adequate equipment.[1]

The selection of a linguist was the simplest, yet the most difficult of all the problems, for there was only one Englishman with a knowledge of Melanesian languages available; this was S. H. Ray, an obscure elementary school teacher in Bethnal Green. His acquaintance had been made through a chain of introductions. In 1887 J. G. Frazer, hearing that a zoologist, then unknown to him, was going out to Torres Straits, wrote to ask him to collect information about totemism, but Haddon would make no promises. On his return he corresponded with

[1] The anthropological work of W. H. R. Rivers is too well known to need any reference. The genealogical method was evolved in the field, also the method of recording string figures (Bibliog. 90), and his magnificent *History of Melanesian Society* (1914) was the climax of the work begun in 1898–9. His sudden death in 1922 was a grievous blow to A.C.H. and to anthropology. In his speech on receiving the first Rivers Medal presented by the Royal Anthropological Institute, January 27, 1925, A.C.H. said: 'One of the things of which I am most proud in a somewhat long life is that I was the means of seducing Rivers from the path of virtue... (for Psychology was then a chaste science)... into that of Anthropology.' Cf. Bibliog. 174.

Frazer on the subject of a paper by Beardmore (Bibliog. 30) and offered him the vocabularies he had collected from various islands. Frazer replied that they were no use to him, and suggested that they should be offered to the Rev. Dr Codrington; but Codrington was just then too much occupied with his *Melanesians* (1891) to spare time for more vocabularies, and recommended S. H. Ray. 'I know no one else in England so well qualified.' No time was lost in applying to Ray, who gladly accepted the offer, and as the result of his work, *A Study of the Languages of Torres Straits* was published by the Royal Irish Academy in 1893 and 1897. Naturally therefore A. C. H. turned to Ray as the only man for the job in the new expedition. But it meant the certain sacrifice of his salary, on which he and his family were dependent, reduction in his pension and probable damage to his prospects. Under pressure the London School Board consented to approve his leave of absence without pay for a year with security of re-appointment on his return.

Haddon never felt quite happy about Ray. The other members of the Expedition all rose high in the world, and he could feel that their work with him had not been unrewarded. But Ray, who had sacrificed more, had no earthly reward; he remained an assistant elementary schoolmaster to the end of his days. The file of correspondence shows the efforts Haddon made to obtain recognition for him, but all in vain, and this man of genius, one of the world's greatest authorities on Oceanic languages, was compelled to earn his living for forty years by teaching elementary arithmetic to large classes of little East-End London boys, snatching what odd hours he could spare for his linguistic work. All that could be secured for him was an Honorary Degree of M.A. at Cambridge (December 12, 1907), and, twenty years later, a pension from the Civil List 'in recognition of his services to literature and the study of ethnology' (cf. Bibliog. 217).

The team was completed with the volunteering of Anthony Wilkin,[1] who, when an undergraduate at King's, had attended Haddon's lectures on Sociology. He joined the Expedition mainly as a photographer and devoted his time to the study of material culture, especially native houses.

C. G. Seligman was a last-minute addition. The party had been made up and Haddon was by no means disposed to enlarge it, but Seligman (an old friend of C. S. Myers) was so persistent that he was reluctantly included. And with what magnificent results! He went out as a medical man with no leanings towards Anthropology. But interest in the natives, primarily pathological, developed more and more widely as was practically illustrated in his work on the Melanesians, the Vedda and the peoples of the Sudan, besides 'researches in archaeology, physical anthropology, material culture, social structure and function, psychology, religion and racial problems', to quote from the admiring and affectionate tribute which A. C. H. wrote for 'Sligs' in the Seligman *Festschrift* (cf. Bibliog. 205).

[1] After his return from Torres Straits he spent some time in North Africa in anthropological and archaeological researches. *Among the Berbers of Algeria* was published in 1900 and *Libyan Notes* (with D. Randall-MacIver) in 1901. He was taken ill and died at Cairo the same year. The Anthony Wilkin Studentship for Anthropology at Cambridge was founded in his memory in 1906.

Raising funds for the Expedition was an uphill task, and it would take too long even to outline the efforts which were necessary before the £1000 on which Haddon had set his heart was in sight. Macalister[1] was appointed Treasurer and contributions were painfully collected. £300 from the Worts Fund was given by Cambridge University, another £300 came from Government, and lesser sums from the Royal Geographical Society, the British Association, the Royal Society, the Government of Queensland and the Royal Dublin Society. A later addition of £175 from the Worts Fund raised the grand total to £1275.

A contribution of equal importance came from the Syndics of the Cambridge University Press, to whose far-seeing wisdom and financial sacrifices in the interests of science Cambridge owes so much, for they agreed to publish the results of the Expedition in a monograph.

The scientific results of this Expedition, the first and most successful of its kind ever launched, appeared in the six volumes of the *Reports* between 1901 and 1935; the popular account is familiar in *Head-Hunters, Black, White and Brown* (1901). It is not necessary therefore, even were space available, to give more than an outline here.

The Expedition left London on March 10, 1898, and reached Thursday Island on April 22, but as no transport was available it was not until the 30th that any of the party were able to start for Murray Island. Then Haddon, Rivers, Ray and Seligman found accommodation of a sort on board the *Freya*, a ketch some 47 feet long, already full of other Europeans, as well as Javanese, Japanese,

[1] A. Macalister, Professor of Anatomy.

Polynesians and Papuans. They had no berths, they slept on deck wrapped up in blankets with improvised pillows, some of them too seasick to move, though the rain pelted down from above and the waves swished up from below, and it took nearly a week of adventure and some dangers to reach their goal. It was just this difficulty of approach that made Murray Island so favourable a spot for study, out of the track of commerce and intrusive civilisation. The rest of the party, after a more comfortable trip in the official schooner, arrived the following week and the work began. It was apportioned as follows: Haddon undertook physical measurements and observations and recorded manners and customs, legends, etc., besides studying decorative art; Rivers, while collecting sociological data, was in charge of experimental psychology; he was responsible for investigation of vision; Myers for smell, hearing and reaction time; McDougall for tactile sensibility and other observations. Seligman studied local pathology and native medicine. Ray devoted himself to linguistics.

Fortunately, owing to Haddon's earlier visit to Murray Island, it was already full of his friends who greeted him with enthusiasm. On Sunday, when he went to the service at the schoolhouse, the congregation waited for him to come out first, and he shook hands with nearly all of them and invited them to come and see photographs after the afternoon service. So crowds turned up:

We had an immense time. To their intense and hilarious delight I showed them some of the photographs I had taken on my last visit.... The yells of delight, the laughter, clicking, flicking of the teeth, beaming faces and other expressions of joy as they beheld photographs of themselves or of friends would suddenly turn to tears and wailing when they saw the portrait of someone since deceased. It was a steamy and smelly performance but it was very jolly to be again among my old friends and equally gratifying to find them ready to take up our friendship where we had left it.[1]

Towards the end of May the pioneer party, Haddon, Rivers, Seligman and Ray, had an opportunity of visiting the mainland, and at Port Moresby a steamer was placed at their disposal for a fortnight and visits were made all along the coast as well as inland, and they did not return to Murray Island until July 20. Kiwai Island at the mouth of the Fly River was visited on September 8 on the way to a five weeks' sojourn on Mabuiag, where the people were more civilised, intelligent and hard-working, combining skilful fishing and industrious gardening with trading and head-hunting, all tending to develop their intelligence. Here the white head-hunter did a good trade, exchanging jew's-harps for skulls, while Rivers perfected his genealogical method, the islanders being far more communicative here than on Murray Island.

In November they left the islands, and Haddon, Seligman and Ray took steamer to Borneo, whither other members of the party had preceded them. While delayed at Kuching (Sarawak), A. C. H. photographed some hundred Sea Dayak fabrics, learning what he could about their patterns, thus laying the foundation of the monograph which was published, with Miss Start's help, in 1936. They coasted round to Limbang and Brunei, being unable to cross the bar at the mouth of the Baram, and then had

[1] *Head-Hunters*, pp. 9–10.

an eleven days' journey in canoes up the Limbang and down the Baram to Claudetown (Marudi). This diversion to Borneo was the result of a pressing invitation from Charles Hose,[1] Resident of the Baram district, who was here their host and organised two up-river trips for them to visit the brown head-hunters of the interior whom he paternally administered. Haddon's full enjoyment of these experiences was spoilt at the time by attacks of malaria, but he always looked back on his visit to Borneo as one of the most delightful of his life, and could never express enough gratitude to Hose for having made it possible. He was especially interested in seeing the way in which this Utopia was administered, all attempts to 'open up' the country and exploit the natives being resisted, however profitable they might be, while the government honestly tried to help the people to govern themselves and encouraged any scheme for the gradual betterment of their condition (cf. *Head-Hunters*, p. 294).

In April 1899 all the members of the Expedition were back in England. Packing cases crowded with specimens arrived in Cambridge and Haddon had enough material to occupy him for many years to come. Unfortunately there was no space where they could even be unpacked. The Museum of Ethnology was then merely a cramped adjunct of the Classical Museum in Little St Mary's Lane,

[1] Hose had gone out as a cadet to Borneo in 1884 and knew and loved his natives and his work as their administrator. He had met A. C. H. once, when on leave, and when he read the notice of the Expedition, he wrote inviting the whole party to visit Borneo, to travel up and down his district seeing what no others had ever seen, putting houses and boats at their disposal, and all expenses paid (cf. Bibliog. 194).

and there was no chance of displaying more than a few special treasures. The Curator, Baron A. von Hügel, devoted much of his time and energy to collecting funds for a museum worthy of the incomparable collections, but this was a slow business, and many of the cases from Torres Straits were stored away for more than twenty years.

In all the affectionate letters to his wife written during his absences in 1888–9 and 1898–9, A.C.H. expressed the hope that he would never have to leave her for so long again. When starting on the earlier occasion he comforted himself by saying 'Kathleen [then a baby of a couple of months] will keep Fanny busy while I am gone', but he never under-estimated the sacrifices she had to make, or the anxieties she had to endure. During the second absence Mrs Haddon had even greater responsibilities and anxieties, both personal and financial. Something went wrong with the Expedition's funds. £150 more was spent on outfit than was anticipated, as Ray and Haddon discovered when they went through the accounts on board 'and they came out correct to 1*d*.', as his diary triumphantly records. Money sent out from home by Macalister, the treasurer of the Expedition, failed to arrive. Mrs Haddon had to borrow from relatives and cable out supplies. Then various posts fell vacant, London, Oxford, Aberdeen. And though she knew that a break with Dublin was imminent and would leave them without a salary, she could not communicate with her husband about applications elsewhere. She sought counsel with the Ridgeways, Michael Foster and Macalister, and the latter urged her to seize the first chance to get out of Cambridge.

All this was very disturbing, as the weekly bulletins from home show, and towards the end they show also the increasing anxiety about Mrs Haddon, senior. She had been in poor health for some time, and now it looked as if she would not live to see her son's return. Should the traveller's anxieties be increased by telling him this or no? The Borneo excursion was only an extra. Could it not be given up or at any rate curtailed? There were 'temporary worsenings', and then the end came on March 30, 1899, and she has to send on the news with what comfort she can add:

Don't grieve overmuch, it is very sad your not being at home, but you are away for duty's sake, not pleasure, and *she* would have been the last to have interfered with that.

This letter ends:

Now my dear, Goodbye again, it wont seem very long when you get this letter before our long separation will be over. I trust there will never be so long a one again. You must expect to find a somewhat grey-haired wrinkled wife on your return! My glass tells me I am much older looking than when you left, so be prepared. (April 7, 1899.)

A. C. H. constantly bore witness to the self-abnegation of his wife, which had made his work possible, and after this long trial he determined to go no more a-roving.

He wrote in his diary:

We slowly steamed away from Thursday Island and the Straits. You can well imagine that it was with mixed feelings that I watched the familiar islands disappearing from view. So much of my life has been bound up in the Straits that I felt as if parting from a personal friend whom I shall probably never see again. Never again do I expect to see the islands or the islanders.

Not many years after his return, however, Haddon was so concerned with the urgency of the work that he was planning a third Expedition, this time on a far more ambitious scale. On his first visit he had seen the rapidity with which not only the old order but all memory of it was dying out; the second visit convinced him that anthropological work in Melanesia must be undertaken at once or the opportunity would be lost for ever.

Posterity will have plenty of time in which to generalize and theorize but it will have scarcely any opportunity for recording new facts. The apathy of our predecessors has lost to us an immense amount of information. Let not this reproach be applied to us by our descendants (*Nature*, XLIII, 1891. p. 270).

In his Presidential address to the Anthropological Institute in 1903 he stressed the importance of immediate action:

Oh! If we could only agree to postpone all work that can wait and spend the whole of our energies in a comprehensive organised campaign and save for posterity that information which we alone can collect!

Three years later he brought the urgency of the matter to the notice of the Royal Geographical Society (Bibliog. 113). He pointed out that there were many anthropological problems requiring investigation in the immediate future, which must be tackled at once or it would be too late.

The presence of Government officials, missionaries, traders and of returned indentured labourers tends rapidly to destroy the old customs. Much has already disappeared in many places; we are yet in time in many others if we do not delay.

106

He had elaborated a scheme of intensive work in special areas by chosen individuals. There was to be first a steady and comfortable steamer with a permanent staff consisting of director, doctor, photographers and typists; investigators would be dropped at suitable spots with the necessary food, trade goods, etc., and collected later when photographers, typists, etc., would assist in making a complete and illustrated record of all available information.

It would be an expensive undertaking but the results obtained would amply justify the expenditure of time, labour and money, and the data thus obtained would constitute a mine of information for present and future generations of students of man.

But it was no use. There was no dearth of volunteers, both men and women, but no wealthy society could be induced to sponsor the scheme, while attempts to obtain Government support were vain. Moreover, it was intimated that even if money were forthcoming it was unsuitable that a man of over fifty should organise and lead such an undertaking. Discouraged at home, Haddon attempted to gain support for his scheme in America, though indifferent as to whether he had any part in it or no. Rivers stressed the urgency of the work in his report to the Carnegie Institution of Washington, pointing out that 'the death of every old man brings with it a loss of knowledge never to be replaced', and Haddon wrote:

The facts and arguments... point clearly to Oceania as being probably that part of the world which most urgently needs ethnological investigation... and a commission for the intensive study of as many portions of that area as possible, combined

107

with an investigation of the more general problems of racial and cultural movements...would confer an incalculable boon on all present and future students of the history of human culture. If this is not attempted very soon the opportunity will pass away for ever.

The year that this was written found A.C.H. unexpectedly and almost unintentionally in Torres Straits again.

3. Percy Sladen Trust Expedition to Papua. 1914

The British Association had arranged to hold their meeting of 1914 in Australia. Haddon was asked to give a paper on the decorative art of New Guinea at Brisbane and he was to receive an honorary degree at Perth. Moreover, he was invited by the Commonwealth to 'pursue anthropological investigation' in Papua after the meeting ended. So having obtained a grant from the Percy Sladen Fund for this purpose he sailed with the advance Overseas party in July, taking his daughter Kathleen with him as assistant and photographer. At this time theories of culture-complexes were abundant and hypothetical routes criss-crossed Oceania, but it was obvious to Haddon that they must remain hypothetical unless the means of migration could be discovered. Migration in Oceania was impossible without canoes; a study of canoes and their distribution was essential before any theories could be put forward. The prime purpose of his trip was therefore a study of the structure, types and distribution of canoes in New Guinea, which led to the survey of the whole of Oceania and to the publication (with J. Hornell) of the three-volume monograph which provides a working basis for subsequent theorising.

News of the outbreak of war reached the B.A. at Adelaide, but this did not seriously interfere with the programme of the Australian meeting, though owing to Government requisitioning of ships all arrangements for the return of the Overseas party were cancelled and alternative plans hurriedly made.

The ship provided by the Commonwealth Government for the Haddons' trip to Papua failed from a different cause, for on their arrival at Melbourne the news was received that it was stranded some 500 miles up the Fly River and was likely to stay there indefinitely. Moreover, no other steamer was available. So plans had to be hastily altered, with the result that A. C. H. found himself back once more in Torres Straits as delighted to see his old friends as they were to see him. After a short stay at Badu and a visit to a stone implement workshop at Yam, they went on to Daru where they met Mr Ryan, an intrepid explorer, Resident Magistrate of the Delta Division, who invited them to his district. They travelled along the coasts noting the junction of Papuan and Melanesian culture, observing, collecting, photographing and sketching, with special reference to canoes, native patterns and native string figures. The account of the trip was not published, but the notes laid the foundations of the *Canoes of Oceania* (1936) and *Smoking and Tobacco Pipes in New Guinea* (in the Press), as well as of K. Haddon (Mrs Rishbeth)'s *Artists in String* (1930).

Chapter V

CAMBRIDGE AND ANTHROPOLOGY

As the name of Tylor is inseparable from Anthropology at Oxford, so is that of Haddon in Cambridge, and the story of his life is also the record of the establishment of the Cambridge Anthropological School.[1] For its beginnings we must return to 1893, when he decided that there was no future for the science in Dublin, and, while continuing his professorial lectures in Zoology there in the winter sessions, settled with his family in Cambridge for the rest of the year. Though his Socialist sympathies disapproved of private property in land, he confessed that he did not live up to his principles, as he bought a house in the cheaper and less academic part of Cambridge beyond the railway, and 'Inisfail', Hills Road, was the Haddon home for the next eighteen years.

At first all seemed promising. Macalister appointed him Lecturer in Physical Anthropology, and this post, though carrying a salary of only £50 a year, was at any rate a beginning; he also gave lectures and courses in Ethnology and Sociology to any who cared to attend. The organisation and collection of funds for the Expedition of 1898 stimulated interest in the University, and there were high hopes of the establishment of a post to

[1] He preferred the title Ethnology rather than Anthropology, but this is not the place for disentangling the two group-names.

welcome his return in 1899; but during his absence W. L. H. Duckworth[1] was appointed to the Lectureship, so it was necessary that some new post should be created and worthily endowed, if Cambridge was not to lose him altogether.

J. G. Frazer, always Haddon's staunch friend, was here the chief organiser, with Ridgeway[2] as a keen supporter and driving force, and in 1899 a Memorial urging the provision of instruction in Ethnology was sent to the General Board of Studies. It contained the following paragraph:

It is an open secret that the University could, without unduly straining its finances, secure the services of one who is not only eminently fitted for the post by training, study and experience, but has already laid the University and science under great obligations by teaching Anthropology in the University without a salary for three years, and by conducting, with marked ability and success, a scientific expedition which has been fruitful in valuable additions to our knowledge...and which has further enriched the University with a large and most valuable ethnological collection. It appears to us that in creating a post such as we have indicated for Professor A. C. Haddon, the University would not merely strengthen itself by adding to its staff a teacher who by his wide knowledge and interests, his indomitable energy, and his infectious enthusiasm would be likely to make Cambridge a centre of anthropological learning and research; it would also perform a very gracious act in thus recognising and rewarding services which have been rendered to it and to science from a disinterested love of know-

[1] Later Reader in Human Anatomy, and Master of Jesus College.
[2] Ridgeway, (later Sir) William, Disney Professor of Archaeology (cf. Bibliog. 185).

ledge, and at personal sacrifices which only those who know Professor Haddon's circumstances can appreciate.

The Memorial was powerfully supported by Heads of Houses and by Heads of Departments, by the Professors of Anatomy, Physiology, Zoology, Geology and Astronomy, besides those of Greek, Archaeology and Fine Arts (Jackson, Ridgeway and Waldstein, good fighters all, for once in harmony). But the result was disappointing. The University 'without unduly straining its finances' established a Lectureship in Ethnology with a stipend of £50 a year (May 1900).

So all the magnificent material brought back to Cambridge[1] had to be stored away in sheds and outhouses to be damaged by damp and ravaged by moth, while Haddon, carrying on his zoological work in Dublin and his ethnological work in Cambridge, had to supplement his insufficient income as best he could, by occasional lectures all over the country, by writing and reviewing, all the while attempting to obtain a post which would enable him to devote more time to the work for which he had sacrificed so much.

The mere physical difficulties of the dual existence were exhausting enough, and even Haddon's strong constitution, subject henceforward to attacks of malaria, felt the strain. Take as example a list of his activities extracted from his diary of the early part of 1900 while the establishment of a post in Cambridge was under discussion.

[1] Forty packing cases were sent home from Torres Straits and New Guinea. 'I am afraid Macalister will be horrified at the amount of freight etc. he will have to pay, especially as I do not know that any funds are available', he writes in his diary.

On January 9 he took the Irish night mail to Dublin.
Lectures, Museum demonstrations, lantern shows, din-
ners, exhibitions of pictures, Council Meetings and
College exams fill up the days before catching the Irish
Mail back again on February 3. In the following week
he had a slight attack of fever and had to cut several
engagements. February 15 was 'a terrible day' with
snowstorms and also with toothache. February 16 was
spent in measuring Borneo skulls and a visit to the
dentist. The next four days he was kept indoors with an
abscess in his jaw, but had to start off again by the Irish
night mail on February 22, giving a lecture to the Folklore
Society in London on his way. He lectured to the Royal
Dublin Society on Borneo on the 23rd, went to the Irish
Literary Theatre (then quite new) and returned by the
mail on the 24th.

It was a time of financial strain too. Money was never
of prime importance to A. C. H.,[1] but he could not live
without it, and family responsibilities were mounting
high. His son Ernest was eighteen and due to leave
Giggleswick and enter Christ's; Mary, two years
younger, was never well in Cambridge and had to be
sent away to a boarding school, whilst Mrs Haddon
herself was not strong, and the labours of house and
garden had to be lightened for her.

A post of £200 a year, which had been confidently

---

[1] Jottings among notes for a lecture on Sociology are characteristic: 'What is living? Man does not live by bread alone.
The cultivation of all his faculties and energies have made Man
what he is and we must not sell our birthright for a mess of
pottage.'

expected in Cambridge, would have made all the difference, but with only £50 life was precarious. In a letter to a friend about this time he wrote:

I certainly have need for all my philosophy as I have had many disappointments in life and now have so much to discourage me. Unless I get something more at Cambridge, I must give up the struggle...give up Anthropology...and return to Dublin. If I could get £200 a year for 5 years, my wife and I are willing to chance it, I would throw up my Dublin post whatever it may be worth (I have reason to believe it will very shortly be augmented) devote myself to Anthropology and Cambridge, and risk what happens at the end of that period. But all this is visionary. Who cares for Anthropology? There's no money in it!

It was this black period to which he somewhat ruefully referred in his speech on his 70th birthday: 'Our University sometimes seems to behave more like the traditional step-mother than like Alma Mater—the Nourishing Mother.'

He felt that he was not wanted in Cambridge. He felt that he was not wanted in Dublin either. He had masses of friends in both Universities, but in neither was there sufficient interest in anthropology to provide a livelihood for him. His Dublin colleagues were anxious to retain him there, but their plans for the bettering of his position and prospects (to which he refers in the letter above) came to nothing. So in the summer of 1901 the Council of the Royal College of Science received with deep regret the resignation of

their distinguished colleague who for 21 years has conducted with eminent ability and zeal the work of the Chair of Zoology.

For many years he has enthusiastically devoted a considerable amount of time to his subject in excess of the official requirements and hence the Council have the greater reason to regret that he has been unable to obtain assurance that the Chair of Zoology will be placed on a more satisfactory basis.

Applications for posts in London and Aberdeen were unsuccessful, but the relinquishing of the Dublin Professorship was made possible by election to a Fellowship at Christ's (February 1901) which provided the bread, if not the butter, for life in Cambridge. True, this was only for three years, but he was willing to risk much in the cause of Anthropology, and 'you might as well starve as an anthropologist as a zoologist' was Mrs Haddon's comment. For the next few years by means of the small but steady profits from his books, *Evolution in Art* (1895) —an unexpected best-seller from the pen of a Professor of Zoology—*The Study of Man* (1898) and *Head-hunters* (1901); by giving University Extension lectures in London and the provinces; and by reviewing for *Nature, The Daily Telegraph, The Morning Post,* and lesser papers, the Haddons were able to 'hold on in Cambridge' as Michael Foster had advised, in hopes of the permanent endowment of Anthropology there. The advice proved sound and the risk well worth taking. In 1904 Haddon succeeded Francis Darwin in a Senior Fellowship at Christ's, which he enjoyed to the end of his life. In the same year came his appointment as Lecturer in Ethnology at the University of London (Martin White Benefaction). In the same year too, Ernest, who had followed his father to Christ's and taken the Natural Sciences Tripos, was appointed Assistant Collector, Uganda Protectorate. So in this year for the first time A. C. H. could afford to pay a secretary-typist a shilling an hour and hand over to her the concocting of syllabuses and lecture notes, the abstracting of papers, the making of lantern slides and the writing of minor reviews. She had no qualifications for the post beyond a smattering of foreign languages, boundless enthusiasm, and a new typewriter, yet he always addressed her as 'Colleague' or 'Comrade' instead of Secretary, and he was as generous with praise as with payment 'in excess of official requirements'.

The same year, 1904, was distinguished by another event, the result of nearly ten years of hard labour. In this year 'the Cinderella of the sciences' was officially recognised for the first time by the establishment (not without some non-placeting) of the Board of Anthropological Studies. Henceforth Anthropology, closely linked with Archaeology, found a place in the official Lecture List, though Haddon had to depend on the generosity of other departments for nearly ten years longer before he had a room of his own in which to lecture or to hold his classes.

Lectures had to be given at odd times in odd corners, and this just suited their unconventional character. There was a friendliness in the discomforts of the temporary building annexed to the Department of Pathology, where A. C. H. described himself as 'ectoparasitic'. He was allowed the use of this as an overflow storeroom, and skulls lined the shelves all round. Here 'the faithful few' sat on upturned packing cases and had occasional picnics after the lectures. Sometimes, half-apologetically, he would charge fees for these courses on the ground that his wife 'wanted a new bonnet', but money-making was never his object and he was always ready to share his vast store of knowledge with any inquiring souls. Many students since distinguished in various departments of life and learning will remember these uncomfortable but stimulating hours.

The support of the Board of Anthropological Studies, with Ridgeway, Rivers and Myers as backers, encouraged Haddon in the furtherance of a scheme which he felt to be of urgent national importance. Here were we, the British nation, with the widest imperial responsibilities in the world, yet providing no opportunity for civil servants, military or naval officers, travellers or missionaries to learn anything about the peoples whom they were to govern or among whom they were to live. Some ten years earlier he had approached the Royal College of Science in London urging that a course in General Anthropology with practical work should be provided there to meet this need, and outlining a comprehensive syllabus: 'It would be a graceful act of recognition of Huxley's work in Anthropology if his College were the first to recognise its importance in so practical a manner and thus supply a long felt want.' But the seed fell on stony ground. There seemed more hope in Cambridge, and Haddon pointed out the necessity for some knowledge of Anthropology, not only for academic study, but for the training of future administrators, since it was obvious that many of the mistakes that they made were due to their ignorance of local customs and religions.

The dangers were recognised by the students themselves, and the Indian Civil Probationers in 1907 asked Haddon for some instruction to be given to suit their needs, a similar course with an altered bias being given to the Sudan Probationers the following year. The innovation attracted attention from outside and the latter course was the result of a request made by Sir Reginald Wingate, then Governor-General of the Sudan. This was the first step towards the official recognition of Anthropology as an essential part in the training of Colonial probationers at Cambridge. Appreciation from outside strengthened the workers within the University, and it was a great step forward when a Diploma in Anthropology was established in 1908. In the following year a Memorandum drawing attention to the growing importance of the subject was sent to the General Board of Studies, which recommended that Dr Haddon, 'an enthusiastic and inspiring teacher and an anthropologist of world-wide reputation', should be appointed Reader in Ethnology with a salary of £200 a year. In spite of a tirade condemning the proposal as 'the most reckless and culpable waste of money that could possibly be imagined' and such adjectives as 'fatuous', 'absurd' and 'preposterous' that enlivened the discussion in the Senate, the appointment was made in October.

This Readership Haddon held for the next sixteen years. During this time he lectured to students for the Diploma and the Tripos (after its establishment), to Colonial Probationers and to incipient missionaries; he also (1903–17) lectured on Anthropogeography in the Geographical Department, thus giving a wider and more human outlook to the subject in Cambridge than it attained elsewhere (Bibliog. 176). It was not until 1923, when he was approaching seventy, that he reduced the number of his ethnological lectures, and he was over seventy when he resigned his post of Reader (in 1925), having borne the whole burden of teaching in the Department with unflagging energy and devotion for nearly a quarter of a century. The Professorship was not established until 1933, by which date Haddon was nearing eighty, and though still more full of vigour than many men of half his years he was ineligible for the Chair which all had hoped to see him fill. He was Emeritus Reader and Honorary Keeper of the New Guinea and Borneo Collections at the Museum of Archaeology and Ethnology until his death, always ready to give help and encouragement in the flourishing Department which, in spite of all difficulties and disappointments, he had succeeded in creating. Difficulties and disappointments had been his lot from early years; success had never come easily, and success measured in terms of *£.s.d.* never at all. His own experiences of discouragements and obstructions deepened his sympathy for others struggling along the same unrewarded paths; he gave substantial aid when he could, and no one who came to him for counsel or advice ever came in vain. His knowledge of the world at large, and of the small world within the University, made him a wise counsellor. He had always encountered lions in his path, and if they could not be faced had learnt to hunt for a way round.

The amount of work that he got through was astonishing. His enthusiastic interest in varied subjects, his eager desire to interest others and win souls for Anthropology, together with a real love of teaching, created a formidable lecturing list and he seldom refused an invitation to spread the gospel. Courses for Cambridge, for London, for University Extension centres, as well as odd lectures here, there and everywhere, had to be planned and written out, at any rate in rough notes, for he never took to a typewriter. The appropriate illustrations or diagrams had to be found, photographed and made into lantern slides. An attic at 'Inisfail' was turned into a dark room and a convenient staircase on to a flat roof made this available for daylight exposures. Hundreds if not thousands of the slides which he presented to the Museum of Archaeology and Ethnology (cf. p. 148) were made with his own hands.

His lectures were nearly as varied as his interests. Some were devoted to his first love, Zoology, and 'Animal Life in a Freshwater Aquarium' recalled the struggles and successes of his youth. Most were anthropological or ethnological, dealing with races and peoples all over the world; sociological, with illustrations from his own observations; or archaeological, on prehistoric skulls or artefacts. There were courses on Art, its Social Functions or the History of Designs, and on Folk-lore; 'Games and Toys' included cat's cradles, and 'Pagan Survivals in Modern Britain' was one of his most popular lectures with the B.E.F. in France.

Inspirations from Le Play, Geddes[1] and Herbertson were moulded into his delightfully original exposition of Anthropogeography, or the Influence of Environment on Man, which culminated in what he called his 'Glory

[1] 'Inspiration' was the word he used to express his debt to 'that versatile and stimulating genius, Patrick Geddes', whose Summer Meetings in Edinburgh the Herbertsons also attended, thus beginning life-long friendships (cf. Bibliog. 189).

Hallelujah' lecture with an unexpected mixture of Paganism and the Gospels. In this he chose eight typical 'environments', deduced the resulting sciences, occupations, types and ideals, human and divine, especially emphasising the Social and Anti-Social developments, which represented Right and Wrong. This was more than a mere lecture, it was a sermon and a confession of faith, and as accretions collected year by year it could not be confined to one hour and might almost take two. But it was worth it, and many who listened to it will be glad to be reminded of its wisdom, its humour and its daring in Fig. 1.[1]

To anyone who did not know him it is difficult to conjure up a sufficiently vivid picture of A. C. H. in his middle period, from 1900 onwards. First impressions were of superabundant vitality, both physical and mental, with a boyish impulsiveness in speech and in action; of a man of the world with a wide experience of its ups and downs, who yet retained many of the gaucheries of the schoolboy. His tall, loosely knit figure, his restlessness, his alert face with keenly observant eyes, and the characteristic shock of black hair now turning white,[2] made him

[1] At Aberystwyth in 1911 the large audience listening to this lecture sat as still as mice for 1¾ hours save for occasional applause, and the students accentuated the vote of thanks at the end with their college yell (cf. Bibliog. 137).

[2] Even in his Dublin days there was a streak of white hair that ran transversely across his head which he called 'the Zone of Zoology' (cf. Pl. IV). He used to attribute this to his experience on his first visit to Torres Straits. On one of the islands there were two springs. Anyone might drink of the lower one, but anyone unworthy who drank at the upper one (as he did) was punished by premature grey hairs.

conspicuous in any company, but he always preferred the background and never really enjoyed prominence in his

ANTHROPO-MORPHIC IDEALS	CYCLOPS	PAN. DRYADS. VEGETATION SPIRIT.	THOR. ACTÆON. ARTEMIS. ANCESTOR CULT.	ODIN. THE GOOD SHEPHERD. MUHAMMED (the inspired camel driver)	BUDDHA. MESSIAH.	DEMETER (CERES). — DIONYSIUS →	PALLAS ATHENE.	POSEIDON. PETER the FISHERMAN and the Apostolic Net. DAGON.
IDEALS	Success in Life. Clang of Bells. Brass Gongs. Tinkling Cymbals.		Idealisation of Death. Glory in the Past. Instability. Trophy of Horns. Valhalla. Plunder.	Idealisation of Life. Faith in the Future. Conservatism. Horns of Honour. Psalm CXLIV, 13.	Rest.	The Promised Land. Bread of Life.	Palm of Victory. Wine and Oil.	
TYPES	Tubal Cain. Lord Kelvin.	Sir Benj. Baker.	Nimrod. Selous.	Sultan as Father of the Faithful. Pope - General Booth. Abraham.	Oom Paul.	Edward VII. Sir Joseph Hooker. Mendel. Burbridge. Darwin.		Nansen.
OTHER OCCUPATIONS	Instrument and Tool Makers.	Engineers. Mechanicians.	Naturalists.	Patriarchal Life. Caravan Traders.	Pioneers. Makers of the West.	Stock Breeders. Gardeners. Doctors.		Explorers. Merchants. Vikings.
SCIENCES	Geology. Mineralogy. Metallurgy. Chemistry.	Forestry. Engineering. Mechanics. Bridges, Roads etc.	Natural History.	Economic Zoology and Botany. Astrology. Astronomy.		Agriculture. Botany. Medicine. Finance. Banking.	Rhetoric.	Astronomy (Nautical Almanac). Navigation. Marine Zoology. Pisciculture.
SOCIAL	MINER (Miners for Stone and Metal)	WOODMAN (Forest)	"Hunter Savages" N.Am.Ind. of Woodlands. Fur Traders. Australians. (Jungle, Bush Veld)	SHEPHERD Kalkhas. Kirghez. Anc. Peruvians. Goths and Vandals. (Prairie, Steppes)	PEASANT I Living on verge of Want or Starvation. Hindus. Boers. Corsicans. (Poor Land)	PEASANT II Chinese. Anc. Mayas. (Rich Land)	PEASANT III Anc. Greeks. Baganda (Banana). Polynesians.	FISHERMAN. Malays. Polynesians. Phoenicians. Norwegians (Vikings). N.W. coast of America.
ANTI-SOCIAL	Greed for Gold (Pay-Dirt). Mammon. Gambling. Treasure on Earth. Serpent Hoard of Niebelungen lied.	Deforester. Destruction of Natural Resources leading to Impoverishment of the Country.	Exterminator Man-Hunter. No future. No forethought. "Muddling through."	Nomad. Sheep stealing. Cattle Lifting. Buonaparte ("the Corsican")	Bandit.	Corner in Wheat. Ringing the Market. Joseph. Wheat Pit of Chicago.	Lotus Eaters. Laissez-Faire.	Pirate Buccaneer. Lawful Trading leading to Illegitimate Trading (Piracy).

Fig. 1. The ethnological interpretation of history.

profession, still less in society. He was a good organiser, taking infinite trouble about practical details, but his lack of fluency and polish detracted from his success as a leader

PLATE IV

Phot. C. M. Thompson

Professor and Mrs Haddon at Inisfail, 1893

when words were wanted rather than works. His leadership was that of a fellow worker, not a dictator.

He was perhaps at his best at his own fireside—by the little gas-fire in his study crowded with books—where he would talk freely, wisely and wittily on any subject under the sun 'except higher mathematics' as he stipulated. The same spirit showed itself on committees when 'an infusion of irrepressible gaiety and quick-witted sallies added zest ...to discussions in scientific circles, in which some humorous comment of his would often cut through a web of sophistication'.[1]

He had no selfish ambitions. Never was a man more generous of his time, his ideas, his work, sketches, photographs, books, and, as far as possible, of his money. He would hand over the accumulated work and notes of years to be turned into a paper or article by some novice whom he wanted to help, claiming no credit. He undertook the editing of other people's books, and wrote prefaces for them; he wrote reviews of obscure books (if he found worth in them) to help obscure authors. The help he gave to his students was unstinted and the sympathetic letters that he wrote them would fill a far larger book than this. He suffered fools patiently though not gladly, but he scarcely concealed his dislike of ostentation and cocksureness, and gloated like a schoolboy at the fall that follows pride.

His religious convictions had developed considerably since his early years, under the influence of Cambridge, science, and the searching for truth. He was commonly lumped in with the generality of anthropologists as pagan,

[1] H. J. Fleure, *Obituary Notices of the Royal Society*, 1940, p. 449.

heathen or agnostic—he never claimed to be anything else.[1] But no one could call him irreligious. He was indeed an unexpectedly regular church-goer, marching the family off every Sunday morning for many years, until Mrs Haddon's deafness interfered with her appreciation of the service, and he lapsed, with a sigh of relief. The Rev. John Kelman,[2] his companion on board ship on a return voyage from Australia, as well as in the self-revealing days with the Y.M.C.A. in France, said 'Haddon has no need of a religion'. And it was one of his (Christianised) Murray Islanders who described him as 'close up alongside God'. Religion, 'the making of gods in our own image', was for him a matter of universal experience, unconfined by sects and creeds; he was interested in all manifestations, and respected all that were genuine. He enjoyed shocking the unco' guid as he enjoyed shocking the unco' prudish, but his lectures on Religion, designed chiefly for workers in the mission field, showed such insight into their special problems and such appreciation of their special susceptibilities that no word struck a jarring note.

These lectures attracted a good deal of attention. He had recognised that just as most of the mistakes made by administrators were due to ignorance of local customs and beliefs (cf. p. 117) so were those of the missionaries, but these were more fatal. He anticipated the modern evangelising approach by pointing out the parallelism

[1] When elected Hon. member of the Cambridge University Nonconformist Union in 1901, he wrote accepting the honour with great pleasure, but added: 'I am not sure that I am really eligible as I do not pretend to conform to anything, scarcely even to Nonconformity.'

[2] Then U.F. Minister in Edinburgh.

between Papuan and Christian thought, though he left it
to others to show how pagan virtues might be encouraged
to develop Christian character.[1]

He was intolerant of cramping conventions whether
religious or secular and this liberating spirit brought him
into conflict with many of the more conservative members
of the University, especially when the question of Degrees
for Women roused their fighting instincts.

He inherited a liberal tradition from his ancestors.
Grandfather Haddon scouted the restrictions of his day
and escorted his sister to Gretna Green for her illegal
marriage (cf. p. 3). John Haddon, the printer, was one
of the first business men in the City to employ women in
his counting-house. A.C.H. was not concerned with
Women's Rights in general, but he was eager to remove
obstructions from their path and to assist their claim to
the Right to Work. What mattered was the quality of the
work done, be the worker man or woman; and an anthropologist is the first to recognise that there are certain
fields of research which are closed to Man.

He invited a woman to lecture in Dublin 'for the first
time in the records of learned and scientific societies in
Ireland'.[2] He rejoiced at the opening of the doors of

[1] In 1902 he gave a joint lecture with the Bishop of New Guinea
(Stone-Wigg) in Caius College Lecture Room showing the
fundamental similarity between ideas of *tabu* and consecration;
laws of compensation and atonement; initiatory rites and con-
firmation; evil spirits and sin, etc. (cf. Bibliog. 95).

[2] *Irish Times*, November 20, 1890. This was Miss Alice Shackleton who helped with the investigation of the sea anemones of
Torres Straits, and after whom *Zoanthus Shackletoni* was named
(cf. Bibliog. 32, 37, 44).

scientific societies to women, usually contriving to take a woman to the first mixed meeting, and it gave him peculiar satisfaction when his daughter Kathleen, after taking her Tripos in 1911, was the first woman to be appointed Demonstrator in the Department in which he had demonstrated for Balfour, a third of a century earlier. He was himself responsible for the unbarring of many doors in Cambridge and for an innovation which gave great offence, the insertion of a woman's name in the List of Lectures in the *Cambridge University Reporter*.[1]

But he was no pro-feminist. He assessed women scientifically and unemotionally, always maintaining that they could do little without men to back them, and he thoroughly enjoyed the gibes for which a mixed class in anthropological subjects gives peculiar scope. In skull measuring he loved to point out, 'Where the female differs from the male it is in being more infantile' and after this had been appreciated—'where the male differs from the female it is in being more ape-like and senile'. And a joke that in mangled form has been the round of the comic papers originated in his class room. He was discussing Sociology and, as happened so often when he was talking about his Torres Straits Islanders, had exceeded his hour.

---

[1] When he was in Australia in 1914–15 he handed over his course of lectures in Anthropogeography to Miss Lilian Whitehouse (then acting as his secretary), though they were still advertised in his name. When in 1920 the lectures were permanently transferred to Mrs Quiggin (an earlier secretary who had collaborated in their production) her name was put down in the Lecture List, a profanation which led to intemperate abuse of women in general and Haddon in particular and its withdrawal for a couple of years.

PLATE V

Garden Party, Christ's College, 1903

Back row: E. HADDON, M. SLATER, C. H. B. EPPS, S. J. FAY, W. G. FEARNSIDES,
C. G. SELIGMAN (self-effacing), MAJOR COOK-DANIEL, I. SLATER,
R. H. RASTALL.

Seated: MRS HADDON, W. BUCKLEY, G. L. ELLES, A. C. H., A. HINGSTON,
H. DREW.

On ground: K. HADDON, A. G. MEADE.

He was describing how in some islands the women, not the men, make the proposals of marriage, when the women students from Girton College, knowing that their cab would be waiting impatiently outside, unostentatiously slipped out at the back. The temptation was too great. He called out, 'No hurry, there won't be a boat for some weeks'.

Throughout his long life he had no hobbies besides his work, and its variety seemed to provide him with all the recreation that he needed. He was always friendly and sociable, joining in a boat-load for the May Races, or giving a 'Departmental Garden-party' for 'the faithful few' and select friends in the beautiful grounds of Christ's College (cf. Pl. V). He enjoyed having people to meals[1] or on visits, just as he enjoyed going out and dining in Hall, but he deplored the waste of time thus spent if it was 'unprofitable' in the language of his early diaries. Every moment of the day was precious and there was never a moment too much, but time could always be found for anyone who wanted help or information and his bookshelves were open to any who cared to consult them.

Sunday afternoons and, after tea, the welcome 'Come up to my study and we'll look at things', are among the most treasured memories of many men and women whose eyes he opened to the fascinations of anthropological by-paths. He would bring out his cases with Mediterranean charms against the evil eye; votive offerings from Irish rag wells; queer currencies from Africa, China or Borneo and skulls from all parts of the world; there was always

---

[1] Home life was necessarily on a simple scale. 'I don't dine: I feed', he would say in inviting a guest.

something new and interesting. The whole house was an inspiration. A Baganda drum summoned to meals, a Borneo basket collected waste paper, the walls were covered with shields, masks and clubs and a skull was a natural ornament of the writing table. One might meet Mary Kingsley and talk fetish; Gomme,[1] and talk folk-lore; Geddes, and listen to anything from town-planning to daffodils; Clodd,[2] and watch demonstrations of social contacts illustrated with paper clips. Travellers from all over the world were welcome as long as they had a smattering of English and something to say about their work; though there are uncomfortable memories of finding A. C. H. in one corner of the room and a distin-guished archaeologist in the other and the growled ex-planation, 'Can't understand his d— language'.

String figures were a peculiarly Haddonian contribu-tion to Brighter Cambridge, and dons and students alike fell under the spell of 'Funiculomania'. 'Toys and Games' was a favourite subject for a lecture even in the Dublin days, and though he could not find ritual significance embodied in our English cat's cradle he could show how such apparently trivial pastimes have ethnological im-portance and can provide clues for theories of culture contact, if not of migration (*Study of Man*, pp. 224–32). Others had collected string figures here and there, but it was Haddon's work to co-ordinate the results, and the joint work of Haddon and Rivers in 1898 (Bibliog. 90) which invented the method of recording and gave signi-ficance to collection. 'You can travel anywhere with a smile and a piece of string' was the Haddon motto, and

[1] Cf. Bibliog. 154.   [2] Cf. Bibliog. 195.

with these 'our champion cat's cradler', as Andrew Lang called him, made friends and collected new figures wherever he went.

On his first visit to Torres Straits he found the children making something similar to our cat's cradles besides intricacies far more complicated, using toes and teeth as well, with moving figures like the Sea Snake, or with stories, like Fighting Men. Some of the simpler ones he met again in America or in Africa. He used to describe how he tried to teach the (late) Katikiro of Buganda the button-hole trick, but he persistently loosed the wrong string, 'cut off his head' and enjoyed the trick none the less. His piece of string, properly doctored by washing and stretching, was his constant companion and one of the secrets of his popularity and his success in gaining the confidence of the natives everywhere, 'for who could suspect of guile a man who sits among the children playing with a piece of string?'[1]

He generously handed over all his collected material to Mrs Furness Jayne, whom he had infected with funiculomania, for her sumptuous volume of *String Figures* published in New York in 1906 (Bibliog. 105). His daughter Kathleen (afterwards Mrs Rishbeth) followed her father's example both in collecting and in co-ordination, tracing the geographical distribution and significance of string figures in *Cat's Cradles from many Lands* (1911) and *Artists in String* (1930).

His literary output after settling in Cambridge was enormous. *Head-Hunters* appeared in 1901, and three volumes of *Torres Straits Reports* filled up the three

[1] Cf. K. Rishbeth, *Cat's Cradles from many Lands.* 1911. p. xvi.

following years. In 1904–5 he started his London University lectures on 'Social Evolution in Oceania', yet *Magic and Fetishism* came out in 1906, two more volumes of the *Reports* were published in 1907 and 1908, and *Races of Man*, his best example of 'pemmican' as he termed it (compressing tough stuff into small space), in 1909. The *History of Anthropology*, another concentrated extract, followed in 1910, and his courageous review of the whole world, *The Wanderings of Peoples*, in 1911. In 1912 the Arts and Crafts volume of the *Reports* was completed.

The collection of material and the writing of these books formed the background of his life; the foreground was occupied with briefer records published in numerous papers (cf. Bibliog. *passim*) and in reviewing. He was referee to the Cambridge University Press and other publishers; he wrote articles and reviews for *Nature*, *Knowledge*, *Man*, *Folk Lore* and less serious periodicals, and in 1903 he became one of the brilliant team which H. W. Nevinson collected for the *Daily Chronicle*, 'the finest set of literary critics then to be imagined' as he proudly described them.[1] They included Bernard Shaw, Lionel Johnson, William Archer and Hubert Bland. Also Edward Clodd,

the friend of genius and the genius of friendship...who could be trusted to write an article on primitive beliefs that surpassed in learning any book he was reviewing. Alfred Haddon, the 'Head-hunter' of New Guinea, was equally good on everything connected with anthropology, primitive ritual and Cat's Cradles.[2]

[1] *Changes and Chances*, 1923, p. 191.   [2] *Ibid*. p. 193.

It was at Clodd's famous Strafford House parties at Aldeburgh that A.C.H. first met Nevinson and many other interesting people, all brilliant conversationalists in the inspiring company of their host, who had an unrivalled power of gathering together around him many of the most conspicuous men, whether of science or of letters, as Nevinson notes later (p. 307). He describes one occasion when, besides Haddon ('one of my best contributors to the literary page'), Thomas Hardy was there (May 30, 1903), recalling the Dorset of his earlier days when life was so much fuller and more various; he talked of the hangman and public floggings with stories of magic as well.

This of course roused Haddon and the rest to scientific discourse on rites of propitiation...how the man who kills pigs cuts out a little piece and eats it raw....For Haddon was there, bubbling over with Primitive Culture——Hugh Clifford, twenty years Governor in the Malay Peninsula...Flinders Petrie with Assyrian face...Clement Shorter, etc. etc.

These were the really 'profitable' days.

Nevinson, with his love of the unusual and the adventurous, his modest belief in his own ignorance' and his eager interest in everything, together with his happy knack of being in the forefront of the world's happenings, was a delightful companion on long walks far down the promontory between sea and river. Both he and Haddon were untiring walkers, and, talking all the while, would return as fresh as when they started. Nevinson describes Haddon at this time with pale brownish face, showing the lines of hard life and hard study from the eyes downward to the corners of the mouth, dark eyes looking at one with penetrating directness, always very much alive, full of curiosity and anxiety to learn. He was always modest and seldom took part in any literary conversation unless some point in his own knowledge were involved. Nevinson adds, 'Even if Meredith and Hardy were in the house I was always glad to have Haddon as companion, for with him I felt no strain'.[1]

A note must be added about Haddon's work as an artist and his lectures and writings about Art, which would have attracted attention apart from his services to Zoology or Anthropology. Probably in his early years, suffering under what are now termed inhibitions, his pen and pencil were his chief means of self-expression, and this form of escape was stimulated and developed by his formal training in preparation for a business career. Sketching came as easily as note-taking: his diaries and his letters are full of illustrations: to see things steadily and to see them whole was for him no mere figure of speech.

When he was in New Guinea on his first visit the native patterns on masks, shields, clubs, tobacco pipes or lime spatulas at once attracted his attention, not only for their artistic merit, but for their value in throwing light on derivations and totem cults, the contact of peoples and the spread of culture. His notes were the foundation of *The Decorative Art of British New Guinea* published by the Royal Irish Academy in 1894, which started people thinking on new lines, as Henry Balfour,[2] himself a

[1] Letter, March 1, 1941.
[2] Curator of the Ethnographical Department, University Museum, Oxford. He had just published his *Evolution of Decorative Art*; cf. Bibliog. 218.

pioneer in the subject and steeped in the Pitt Rivers tradition, admiringly recorded.

Proceeding from the particular to the general, as was his way, Haddon produced in the following year the more popular exposition *Evolution in Art as Illustrated by the Life-history of Designs* (1895), with illustrations from all over the world. He brought the methods of the biologist into the study of art and traced the evolution of patterns made by simple peoples in their local setting. Avoiding speculation as far as possible, he collected the evidence and let the facts speak for themselves. Just as in biology the fundamental aphorism is *Omne vivum e vivo*, 'All life from life' so, given sufficient material, patterns can be traced back as the result of a long series of variations from a quite dissimilar original (p. 308).

He was always hoping to find time for a new edition of this book, for which he was accumulating material throughout his life, but more pressing work occupied him until the end.

Writing was not for A. C. H. a mere vacation exercise; vacations were spent far more practically and energetically in collecting fresh material. One year he would be digging for neolithic artefacts in Ireland or in Cornwall; another he would be visiting museums on the Continent (and there were few with which he was not familiar), or dashing over to Canada and the United States, 'tremendously impressed with American energy and enthusiasm' (cf. Bibliog. 89). There were meetings of the British Association when he was sure to be on several committees, and he was President of Section H in Belfast in 1902 and in South Africa in 1905.

Like Sir Thomas Herbert (1665)

> He travel'd not with Lucre sotted,
> He went for Knowledge and he got it,

but on rare occasions Knowledge and Lucre were pleasantly combined. America supplied both the opportunity and the funds. At the invitation of G. A. Dorsey of the Field Columbian Museum, Chicago, Haddon lectured there and at other American centres in 1900, Chicago alone offering twice the amount that 'poor blind Cambridge', as his American friends called her, was able to contribute in a year. In 1906 (mainly owing to the efforts of W. Z. Ripley) he was invited to give the Lowell lectures in Boston (at 2 dollars a minute as he calculated); and in 1909, when he lectured at Seattle on the evolution of culture round the Pacific, the terms were generous enough to enable him to take his wife and both daughters with him.

On these occasions he enjoyed some of the most interesting and instructive experiences of his life, sweating in the sweat-house and dancing in the Medicine Pipe dance with Blackfeet Indians in Montana; and helping to celebrate the Morning Star ceremony with the Pawnee in Oklahoma. He visited the Blackfeet in company with E. S. Curtis, artist and photographer, who was living among them and whom they recognised as their friend and well-wisher. It happened that Little Plume, an old Piegan chief, was making a sweat-house for another old man, Tearing Lodge, and both Curtis and Haddon were invited to join in the ceremony.[1] The sweat-house was

---

[1] The account is condensed from an unpublished MS. and is a good example of Haddon's mental capture of salient features, note-taking being forbidden.

a framework of willow boughs some eight feet by six, about four feet high in the centre, covered with cloths and blankets. A hole was scooped out in the middle and the surrounding space carpeted with sage-grass. A wood fire for heating the stones was made close by. Ablutions, draughts of water, thurification and ceremonial smoking preceded the sweating and prayers were continuous. The heated stones were brought in, water was poured over them and when the entrance was closed the heat was intense. 'It was a novel sensation to be one of seven nude men squatting closely side by side in the dark, steaming with perspiration and being constantly parboiled by puffs of steam.' After what seemed like a long time a little fresh air was let in and cool water given to all to drink. Then prayers were resumed, more water was thrown on to the stones and the heat became insufferable, though relief could be obtained by holding the head low, almost on the ground. When the ceremony was over he bathed in an adjacent stream and felt very pleasing after-sensations, purified and exalted in body and mind.

Some time before this, Little Plume had been ill and his youngest brother, Yellow Kidney, had vowed a Medicine Pipe dance if he got well, which he did. This was also a religious rite, with prayers and incense, the opening of the sacred bundle, ceremonial smoking of the ancient pipe, therapeutic painting with red and black paint, drumming, songs and dances.

Haddon had promised Little Plume that he would take part in the dance, but when it came to his turn he was warned that it would be very unlucky if he tripped up or let any of the feathers fall off the pipe stem and he was thankful that he was able to get through his performance without mishap. This trip also provided an experience of a very different character. He was camping with Dalby, one of Curtis's investigators, at Steveston, B.C., where the West-Coast Indians collected for the salmon canning. The police organised a raid on the Chinese barracks of one óf the canning companies where illegal practices in connection with *fan-tan* were suspected, and the white visitors were pressed into the King's service. Haddon excused himself from taking part in the actual raid, owing to his short-sightedness, but volunteered to guard the sixty-six prisoners that were taken, and he was on duty up to 4.30 a.m. and all day from 8.30 to 6, not undressing for three days. There were rumours that the Chinese were going to raid the gaol, and once, when the lights went out, there was a very uneasy quarter of an hour, standing with his companion with a gun pointed at the cells. 'This is not exactly what I came out for to do' he wrote in a letter home; 'instead of Indian Ethnology I have had a practical lesson in Sociology. . . . But I am having a great time, full of new experiences, some of which will be useful for teaching and others for yarning.' He carefully preserved the chit for $12.50 received for services rendered.

On another occasion, together with G. A. Dorsey, who was a recognised member of the Pawnee tribe, he took part in the Morning Star ceremony at Oklahoma. About a score of men were present, and there were speeches, invocations, songs, shaking rattles, and dances, with ceremonial smoking, and handling of the sacred bundle with the tribal 'medicine'. The ritual was continued hour after hour with great solemnity; occasionally members of the audience would relieve their feelings by ejaculations of *Nawa*, 'It is well', reminding Haddon of evangelical meetings at home with interjections of 'Amen' or 'Bless the Lord'; but the atmosphere was throughout one of sedate decorum. About midnight there was an interval for food, then the ritual was resumed and special purification was necessary before the sacrifice, formerly of a maiden, but now of corn. Later on wooden bowls of soup and buffalo horn spoons were handed round to all, and ribs of beef (representing the departed bison) which they held in their hands, tearing off the flesh with their teeth. A meat offering and the wrapping up of the sacred bundle concluded the ceremony just before dawn.

Visits to America, enjoying the unstinted hospitality of his many American friends, delighting in their sumptuous museums and their enthusiasm for Anthropology, with rare opportunities such as those described above for insight into Indian life and customs, were among his happiest memories. He would return stimulated and encouraged, only to be depressed again by the academic apathy and lack of financial support at home.

Chapter VI

CAMBRIDGE AND ANTHROPOLOGY

The year 1911 marks a turning point in the Haddon history. Up to that time had been a period of *Sturm und Drang*, of hard labour, plain living and high thinking, but the thinking always interrupted by the necessity of earning enough to provide a first class education for the three children. As the children emerged one by one, parental responsibilities slackened. Ernest entered the Civil Service in Uganda in 1905. Mary married in 1910. Kathleen left College and was appointed Demonstrator in Zoology in 1911. All this relieved the financial strain, and the parents were able to contemplate a little more comfort in their old age. Mrs Haddon's health had not been satisfactory for many years and her increasing deafness inclined her to devote herself more and more to house and garden. But the house was crowded with books and treasures, spreading from the small study along the passages and into bedrooms,[1] and the garden was a narrow overlooked strip.

A move was therefore desirable and lessened liabilities made it financially possible, so in 1911 a larger house was

[1] Mary's marriage vacated a bedroom which was at once pounced upon for skulls, books and a supplementary workroom, and Kathleen suspected her father of wanting to marry her off to secure another room.

taken at the West End of Cambridge at 3 Cranmer Road, where there could be a real bookroom as well as a study, and where there was a garden full of delights with ample space for a tennis court (destined for grandchildren) from which in the course of a few laborious years A.C.H. eliminated every intrusive weed. The addition of a verandah some years later provided a delightful semi-out-of-doors room for work and for meals.

Here A.C.H. settled down to tackle the last volumes of the *Torres Straits Reports*. But work was interrupted by the trip to Australia and New Guinea as already described (pp. 108–9), and soon after his return he found himself engaged in field work of a very different nature.

> When I gave my address at the St Louis Exposition in 1904 I had to speak against the mimic warfare of the Siege of Gettysburg in an adjacent booth and hard work it was at times to make myself heard. Little did I think that the time would come when I should have to lecture against the noise of guns in the greatest of all wars.

This was written on March 3, 1917, at the Y.M.C.A. headquarters in France where A.C.H. was thoroughly enjoying himself, getting through an amount of work, both as lecturer and as 'counter-jumper' in the canteen, that would have knocked out most of the 'over 60's'. He describes a typical day.

> Arrived at Christ's Hut[1] in a hail-blizzard, settled down, had tea, and then gave a lecture on New Guinea Cannibals to about 150 men. It went off very well. Then a very busy time serving

---

[1] Christ's Hut was in a dug-out captured from the Germans in the spring of 1917, and shortly afterwards 'Patronised by H.M. the King' (*Red Triangle*, July 20, 1917, p. 651).

at the counter, cocoa, cake, biscuits, tobacco, candles, matches, etc. etc. It's very puzzling at first with English, French and Belgic money of all denominations, all in a terrible rush. Supper at 9 p.m. and bed about 11. There was a regular gale in the night, the wind howled like heavy motor cars rushing past and in the morning the ground was thick with snow. It drove into the passage and into one of the bedrooms, a little dripped on to my bed. But there were plenty of blankets and wraps so I was warm and cumfy and had a really good night. There was some firing, but it was really too bad a night for anything.

Some of his time was spent in 'Cambridge House', some 500 yards from the firing line, reached by scrambling over duckboards along a communication trench:

All is low, dark and grimy, and rats overrun it at night. Troops reeking with the filth of battle frequent it at all hours of the day and night, for it is never closed. The hellish orchestra of war is almost constantly playing with its discords of booms, bangs, crumps, crashes, rat-tat-tats, whizzes, screechings and whines. The body is wearied with constant standing and serving in a stuffy smoky atmosphere, by unappetising food and wakeful nights, the brain becomes deadened and lethargic with the noises and vibrations. But the spirit overcomes it all and with a smile and cheery voice all are welcomed and several hundreds are served all night long. For weeks on end the devoted workers toil on, and for a well-earned rest retire to the nearest village and sleep in a damp cellar in a shelled building. (Cf. Bibliog. 159.)

In April things were getting too hot at the Front and all supernumeraries were sent home, but he writes gleefully:

This does not affect me as I am a 'Worker' and what lectures I give are incidents.... Personally I find that gun-firing stimulates me like the drum-beating of savages, and so far I have not felt the slightest fear. I feel I have now got to my job and I am quite satisfied and happy.

And in a letter in June after very trying heat, constant duty at the hut, and 'pretty continuous bombardment day and night', he adds:

It is good to be alive and take however humble a share in these great events. It is you at home who need cheering up, who have to bear the hardships and the long weary strain of the war. I sometimes feel quite selfish in being out here.... The Front is the place for good spirits.

In June and July he can't think what is coming over him, he actually enjoys being lazy. 'I haven't even wanted to do anything, and do not feel restive. I seem to do nothing but eat and stroll about with the Y.M.C.A. folk. I hope I do not get permanently lazy.' He was still giving a lecture a day at different centres, writing articles for publication, and asks for more books to be sent out for review as he has so much time for 'desultory reading'.

Towards the end of August, however, he consulted a doctor who advised his return home.[1] 'I have certainly felt the emotional strain and I want to be in good working order before term begins.' So he was back in Cambridge early in September and took his wife off to Hunstanton 'as she needed a good holiday'. But there was no holiday for himself. There were fewer students to lecture to until the war was over, but shortly afterwards he was called on for work of a more strenuous nature in connection with the Museum of Archaeology and Ethnology.

[1] He had had some internal trouble which necessitated a slight operation in 1915 and recurred in 1917, needing a further operation in 1919.

Baron A. von Hügel, Curator of the Museum (cf. Bibliog. 192), was obliged by illness to give up his work during 1920. Haddon was then well over the age at which most men seek relief from their heavier labours; he was moreover only lately recovering from a series of operations. Nevertheless, while still carrying on the duties of the Readership, he took over the superintendence of the Museum during the Baron's illness and was appointed Deputy-Curator on his resignation.

The Museum had moved into its new and enlarged quarters in Downing Street in 1913, but was still in course of arrangement. Under Haddon's superintendence much that had not seen the light for a score of years emerged from dusty packing cases, and through the labours of himself in overalls in the van, and a band of devoted volunteers, he created a working museum for anthropological and archaeological students. In his view, frequently insisted on, a museum should always be a working museum; not (as is too common) a collection of 'curios' but a group of related objects each with a tale to tell.[1] So, during his brief curatorship, he introduced this conception to Cambridge, arranging special Student-series side-shows, and made the Museum and the material

[1] Some thirty years earlier he had stated his views: 'A museum has at the present day quite a different object from what it had in the past. The distinction can be put quite succinctly by an analogy; most of the older museums bear the same relation to modern museums that dictionaries do to textbooks... giving the least amount of instruction beyond the bare fact of the existence of given objects... while if properly conducted [museums] afford the most interesting and vivid means for conveying information.' Horniman Museum, Forest Hill, London, to which he was adviser, best embodied his conception of what a Museum should be. (Cf. Bibliog. 92, 101, 104.)

culture which it illustrates essential factors in ethnographical and also in geographical work.

The creation of the Museum Library is a characteristic example of Haddon's energy and determination and of his way of getting a thing done in spite of apathy or passive resistance.

The whole story is probably known only to the chief conspirator from whom the following account was obtained. The Museum had always housed the collections of the Cambridge Antiquarian Society, and also the wonderful, but gappy, collection of books gathered by the Baron, but few knew of their existence, and no one could say whether it was one library or two. Recommendations about it had frequently been made, but no one had the interest, leisure, or determination to tackle it seriously. The Board of Anthropological Studies appointed a Committee which apparently never met, and Dr Haddon, growing impatient, had the books quietly gathered together, arranged, catalogued and adequately housed in part of a large hall on the ground floor previously used as a lumber room. At the next Board Meeting he pressed the Committee to say how far they had got in their duties and after they had been compelled to confess that nothing had been done, he led them triumphantly into the library —in spite of its make-shiftiness it was one of which any Department might well feel proud—and after a few tense moments they burst into roars of laughter.[1]

[1] Charles Sayle of the University Library was a helpful co-worker in the secret scheme, but most of the hard labour, sorting, cataloguing and arranging, was done by Miss E. S. Fegan, well known in England and ·West Africa for her librarianship, her educational work and her all-round efficiency.

When with the acquisition of more rooms the Museum was able to move the books into worthier quarters, it was appropriate that the collection which he had thus successfully inaugurated, and to which he had so largely contributed, should be called the Haddon Library. Here the portrait of its founder with a New Guinea skull in his hand, one of the best pictures ever painted by de László, looks down from the end of the room so that (as Professor E. H. Minns said at the time of the opening) 'readers shall have there the ikon of their patron saint' (cf. Frontispiece).

The Readership was resigned, as has been recorded, in 1925, partly because Haddon felt that he had 'done his bit', partly because he felt that a younger man should take charge of the department; but mainly because he wanted to get on with his own work, an immense amount of which lay temptingly before him. There were the *Torres Straits Reports* to be finished before he felt free to devote himself to the three great monographs that awaited his leisure— one on Oceanic canoes, one on New Guinea tobacco pipes, and one on Bornean fabrics. Moreover, he was only waiting to clear all these out of the way before rewriting his *Evolution in Art* for which he had collected a mass of material. This was a brave programme, the greater part of which was successfully accomplished. The publication of the *Reports* had begun 'with startling rapidity' as one reviewer expressed it, five volumes being published between 1901 and 1912. Then came the War. But the volume on General Ethnography which was to sum up the whole was delayed by other causes as well. Haddon was continually in touch with administrators, missionaries,

PLATE VI

Phot. Cambridge Daily News

Golden Wedding

(21 *September* 1931)

travellers and collectors, and material was constantly accumulating. Instead of regarding Torres Straits and New Guinea as his special preserve, he was always eager that others should work there and all his knowledge was at their service.[1]

Six stout volumes of 300 to 400 pages sound adequate for the description of the sparse population of these small islands, 'few in numbers but rich in interest', but the editor was sadly conscious of the imperfections of the record and he never felt able to say the last word. 'The first shall be last and the last first' applies to the *Reports*, as to other human ambitions. Vol. I was the last to be published, thirty-four years after vol. II, which was the first to appear. But vol. II still lacks the section on the physical characters of the natives, and the dust cover of vol. I implies that it will not now be completed.

Two milestones stand out in Haddon's later period—the celebrations of his 70th and his 80th birthdays in 1925 and 1935. Ridgeway had intentionally prepared the ground for some commemoration in his review of Haddon's services to Anthropology at the opening of the Cambridge Anthropological Club in May 1922, and he and Rivers had discussed possibilities, but nothing definite was planned. An entirely new turn was given to vague aspirations when Miss E. S. Fegan boldly approached Sir William and incited him to call a meeting in Caius

[1] Notably was this the case with Dr Gunnar Landtman (later Professor of Sociology at Helsingfors, Finland), who startled and delighted Haddon by appearing in Cambridge and saying, 'I will go anywhere in the world you like to send me'. So he was sent off to Daudai and the Fly River to trace affinities between the islands and the mainland. (Cf. Bibliog. 186.)

Combination Room in May 1924, 'to consider an appropriate way of celebrating Dr Haddon's 70th birthday'. This was followed by a series of meetings, with Ridgeway in the chair, and a local committee was formed to discuss ways and means. A dinner in Christ's College Hall, with speeches, was obvious and inevitable, but for the more permanent memorial opinion was divided between a volume of essays and a portrait. After some discussion a portrait was amicably agreed on, and the artist selected. De László, who could refuse an offer of a thousand guineas or so, was not only willing but eager to undertake the commission for a fraction of the sum, and in the end painted three separate portraits, one (in Doctor's scarlet gown) for Christ's College, as commissioned, one for the Museum of Archaeology and Ethnology (reproduced in the frontispiece), and a third for the Haddon family.[1]

Far more heated discussions, with agitated notes between chairman and secretaries, were caused by the daring proposal that women subscribers to the Portrait Fund should be admitted to the Dinner. It was assumed by the chairman that Mrs Haddon and the two daughters should be permitted to view the proceedings in proper

---

[1] The order was really reversed. The 'family portrait' was begun on April 15, the Museum one on the 19th and the College portrait last, on May 7. 'Keep on your happiest expression, and *don't* get your hair cut', pleaded Ridgeway. De László, painter of kings and queens, came to Cambridge to see Dr Haddon; one glance was enough, and an extraordinary friendship was struck up between the two men. De László always considered the Museum portrait of the head-hunter with a skull in his hands as one of his best, 'but then I had a delightful sitter'.

obscurity from the gallery, and to those familiar with Cambridge politics there was piquancy in the suggestion that the profane innovation of women dining in Hall should be inaugurated with Ridgeway at the head of the table. Haddon had never interested himself in University politics, still less in University party-politics with the feuds thereby engendered, which were, to one of Ridgeway's Irish temperament, the salt of life. So the two, who had been friends from the Dublin days, often found themselves on opposite voting lists in Cambridge, and what seemed to Haddon a matter of opinion was to Ridgeway a matter of offence. This was particularly the case with the question of women's degrees. Haddon was in favour of emancipation. Ridgeway strongly opposed. This and other University differences had even led to an estrangement which lasted for several years, so it was no slight test of Ridgeway's sincere affection for Haddon when he had to assent to the proposal made in accordance with the well-known wishes of the chief guest, that women should be admitted to the dinner on equal terms with men.

The birthday dinner was a great success, partly some said on account of the novelty of feminine infiltration, but mainly on account of the permeating spirit of friendliness. Haddon himself expressed it when he recalled how fifty years before he had 'entered Christ's Hall knowing nothing and nobody; tonight it is full of my friends'; and later in his speech he gave the clue to universal friendliness:

In the course of a somewhat long life and in going to and fro upon the earth and visiting many cities of men, I have learned the great lesson that one can practically always rely upon the goodness of human nature.

Or, to quote his less academic advice, 'Treat a man as a gentleman and you'll find him a gentleman: treat him like a dam' nigger and he'll behave like one.'

Tributes of affection and esteem poured in from the ends of the earth and Haddon was unaffectedly surprised at their warmth and volume. Preserved among the souvenirs of the dinner is a list made out in his own hand of the twenty-three different countries from which these messages were received.

This spirit of friendliness had another concentrated outburst ten years later and it is characteristic both of the man and of his work that this commemoration was of the gifts that he had given to the University rather than of gifts that he had received. Besides his unrivalled collections from New Guinea, Torres Straits and Borneo, collections of skulls, collections of stone implements and anything that his discriminating eye had picked out, or his friends had given him in his travels over the world, he had presented his collection of lantern slides and a vast number of photographs. It was a happy suggestion, brought to fruition by Mr Louis Clarke, then the Curator of the Museum, that all these photographs, together with the originals of the lantern slides, should be uniformly reproduced, mounted and catalogued and stored in a suitable case for reference. This case containing some ten thousand photographs was formally presented to A.C.H. at the birthday tea at the Museum (graced by a cake with eighty candles) and formally presented by him to the University. It now stands in the Haddon Library 'a permanent record of his life's work and universal interests' (*Man*, 1940, 123).

The next five years were spent mainly in completing the monographs. 1935 saw the publication of the final volume of the *Reports*, and also of the brilliant collaborative effort (with Julian Huxley and A. M. Carr-Saunders) of *We Europeans*. In 1936, with the help of Miss L. E. Start, *Iban or Sea Dayak Fabrics*, much of the material for which had been collected nearly fifty years earlier, at length saw the light; and in the same and following years *Canoes of Oceania*, in collaboration with J. Hornell, was published by the Bernice P. Bishop Museum in Honolulu. There were also minor articles, reviews, introductions (some not yet published) and the last obituary notice, that of Sir Hubert Murray, patron of the first expedition to Torres Straits, was written in 1940 (Bibliog. 219).

Edward Clodd, when congratulating Haddon on attaining the age-limit fixed in the Psalms, had complained of David's arbitrary selection of three-score years and ten, adding characteristically 'But then, consider what a fast life he had lived'. Haddon's life was ascetic in comparison and his four-score years sat lightly on him. A neighbour, commenting on his perennial youth, added 'He was the only man I ever knew who habitually tumbled *up* stairs. My wife and daughter used to say that when they heard on my staircase a sound like a cascade of books, they knew Dr Haddon was charging up to see me in my study.' An anonymous admirer wrote

> When first we knew you, we were apt to stare
> To see a youthful head with such white hair;
> Now on the contrary we're prone to start
> To see white hair with such a youthful heart.

The years pressed more heavily on Mrs Haddon, who, after prolonged battling with ill-health, died in 1937. Kathleen Rishbeth and her children had shortly before this come to make their home in Cranmer Road, bringing sweetness and light with them, and Ernest, retired from Uganda, settled next door. Life was as full and work as interesting as ever, but the strain was slackening and the sunset light was mellow. Haddon still spent much of his time at the Museum of Archaeology and Ethnology where he was a source of information and inspiration to all fellow-workers. It was a great deprivation when rheumatism and lumbago prevented his visits in the winter of 1939–40 and he was confined to the house. He was finishing off his monograph on *Smoking and Tobacco Pipes in New Guinea*, and as the weeks passed it vexed him that he was so easily tired and was unable to concentrate for long. Indeed, he would often drop asleep over the pages. Miss Fegan, who had been his official and unofficial secretary and general factotum on and off for 25 years, was home on leave from West Africa and devoted her time to the final editing. It was a great satisfaction to him when she could announce that it was ready for submission to the Royal Society (which undertook its publication) just before he died.

As spring advanced his weakness increased. Occasionally when feeling his dependence on daughters, Miss Fegan, housemaid or nurse he would murmur with a sigh, 'No life for a man', but he was uncomplaining and death came almost imperceptibly on April 20, 1940, a few weeks before his 85th birthday.

It is perhaps too soon to see the full result of Haddon's

work and assess his contribution to the world of science, but it was no small achievement for a man with so little encouragement, whose whole life had perforce to be spent in teaching, to become one of the foremost ethnologists of our time. It may be that his work as a teacher was even greater and will be more enduring than his work as a scientist, for he had the gift of inspiring others and his students have carried his ideals with them to the ends of the earth. A distinguished pupil (one of 'the faithful few' of the packing-case era, pp. 116–7) wrote 'In all the work I do my one aim is to carry on as well as I can the tradition and spirit of your teaching and example in Cambridge. I am glad my work is successful because I think it will give you pleasure and because you may claim that the success is yours.' And another, equally distinguished, 'trying to say "Thankyou" for all you have done for me. . . . I always remember what you told me when I tried to say something of the kind before, that the only way was to help somebody else on, though I shall never be able to do as much for anyone as you have done for me.' He gave of his best to all alike, worthy or unworthy. An obscure pupil records, 'I owe all the chief interests and pleasures of my life to your kindness in teaching a very ignorant Extensionist in 1899'; and another, 'On reflection I find that anything I have done worth doing has been prompted by you'.

His academic distinctions were many, his degrees and medals not a few;[1] but he was as proud of his students'

[1] From Paris, Berlin, Vienna, Stockholm, Helsinki, Rome, India, Batavia, Australia, New Zealand, New York, Washington and Philadelphia. Cf. *Man*, 1940, 139. p. 100.

successes as of his own. His Anthropology might be called Philanthropology. His great service to Science, for which he will always be famous, was to lay the foundations and to build the framework of Anthropology well and truly on sound scientific principles; his service to humanity was to show that 'the proper study of Mankind' is to discover Man as a human being, whatever the texture of his hair, the colour of his skin or the shape of his skull.

SELECT BIBLIOGRAPHY

A full list containing over 600 items, collected by Miss E. S. Fegan, is deposited in the Museum of Archaeology and Ethnology, Cambridge.

(1) 1880. On the extinct land-tortoises of Mauritius (*Trans. Linn. Soc. (Zool.)* (2), II, p. 155).

(2) Air-bladder of herring (*Nature*, XXII, p. 534).

(3) The Greek fret (*Nature*, XXIII, p. 9).

(4) 1881. On the stridulating apparatus of *Callomystax Gagata* (*J. Anat. Physiol.* XV, p. 322).

(5) 1882. Notes on the development of Mollusca (*Quart. J. Micr. Sci.* N.S. XXII, p. 367).

(6) 1883. On budding in Polyzoa (*Quart. J. Micr. Sci.* N.S. XXIII, p. 516).

(7) 1884. On the generative and urinary ducts in chitons (*Proc. Roy. Dublin Soc.* N.S. IV, p. 223).

(8) 1885. On a new species of *Halcampa* from Malahide (*Proc. Roy. Dublin Soc.* N.S. IV, p. 396).

(9) (with G. Y. Dixon) Structure and habits of *Peachia hastata* (Gosse) (*Proc. Roy. Dublin Soc.* N.S. IV, p. 399).

(10) Note on the blastodermic vesicle of mammals (*Proc. Roy. Dublin Soc.* N.S. IV, p. 536).

(11) Note on *Halcampa chrysanthellum* (Peach) (*Ann. Mag. Nat. Hist.* (5), XVI, p. 523).

(12) 1886. Preliminary report on the fauna of Dublin Bay (*Sci. Proc. R.I.A.* (2), IV, p. 523).

(13) Note on *Halcampa chrysanthellum* (Peach) (*Proc. Roy. Dublin Soc.* N.S. V, p. 1).

(14) 1886. Report on the *Polyplacophora* collected by H.M.S. *Challenger*. Part XLIII.

(15) First report on the marine fauna of the south-west of Ireland (with others) (*Sci. Proc. R.I.A.* (2), IV, p. 599).

(16) 1887. *An Introduction to the Study of Embryology.* London.

(17) Suggestion respecting the epiblastic origin of the segmental duct (*Proc. Roy. Dublin Soc.* N.S. V, p. 463).

(18) Note on the arrangement of the mesenteries in the parasitic larva of *Halcampa chrysan-thellum* (Peach) (*Proc. Roy. Dublin Soc.* N.S. V, p. 473).

(19) On two species of Actiniae from the Mergui Archipelago (*J. Linn. Soc.* (Zool.), XXI, p. 247).

(20) 1888. Second report on the marine fauna of the south-west of Ireland (with W. S. Green) (*Sci. Proc. R.I.A.* (3), I, p. 29).

(21) 1889. A revision of the British Actiniae. Part I (*Sci. Trans. Roy. Dublin Soc.* IV, ser. II, p. 297).

(22) Contributions to the anatomy of fishes (with T. W. Bridge) (*Proc. Roy. Soc.* XLVI, p. 309).

(23) Zoological notes from Torres Straits (*Nature*, XXXIX, p. 285).

(24) On some former customs and beliefs of the Torres Straits islanders (*Nature*, XL, p. 633).

(25) 1890. The ethnography of the western tribe of Torres Straits (*J. Anthrop. Inst.* XIX, p. 297).

(26) Report on the Actiniae dredged off the south-west coast of Ireland (*Sci. Proc. R.I.A.* (3), I, p. 370).

(27)   The newly hatched larva of *Euphyllia* (*Proc. Roy. Dublin Soc.* N.S. VII, p. 127).

(28)   The affinities of *Heliopora caerulea* (*Nature*, XLII, p. 463).

(29)   Manners and customs of the Torres Straits islanders (*Nature*, XLII, p. 637).

(30)   Notes on Mr Beardmore's paper on the natives of Mowat, Daudai, New Guinea (*J. Anthrop. Inst.* XIX, p. 466).

(31)   Legends from Torres Straits (*Folk Lore*, I, p. 47).

(32)   1891.   A revision of the British Actiniae. Part II (with A. M. Shackleton) (*Sci. Trans. Roy. Dublin Soc.* IV, ser. II, p. 609).

(33)   The anthropometric laboratory of Ireland (with D. J. Cunningham) (*J. Anthrop. Inst.* XXI, p. 35).

(34)   The Tugeri head-hunters of New Guinea (*Internat. Arch. Ethnogr.* IV, p. 177).

(35)   Art and ornament in British New Guinea (*Nature*, XLIII, p. 188).

(36)   Throwing sticks and canoes in New Guinea (*Nature*, XLIII, p. 295).

(37)   Reports on the zoological collections made in Torres Straits (with A. M. Shackleton) (*Sci. Trans. Roy. Dublin Soc.* IV, ser. II, p. 673).

(38)   1892.   Contributions to the anatomy of fishes (with T. W. Bridge) (*Proc. Roy. Soc.* LII, p. 139).

(39)   On the value of art in ethnology (*Nature*, XLVI, p. 432).

(40)   1893.   Contributions to the anatomy of fishes (with T. W. Bridge) (*Phil. Trans. Roy. Soc.* B, p. 63).

(41)   1893.   A study of the languages of Torres Straits
               (with S. H. Ray) (*Proc. R.I.A.* (3), II,
               p. 463).

(42)   Studies in Irish craniology. Part I. Aran
               Islands, Co. Galway (*Proc. R.I.A.* (3), II,
               p. 759).

(43)   The ethnography of the Aran Islands (with
               C. R. Browne) (*Proc. R.I.A.* (3), II, p. 768).

(44)   Descriptions of some new species of Actiniaria
               from Torres Straits (with A. M. Shackleton)
               (*Sci. Proc. Roy. Dublin Soc.* N.S. VIII,
               p. 116).

(45)   British New Guinea (*Nature*, XLVII, p. 414).

(46)   A wedding dance-mask from Co. Mayo (*Folk
               Lore*, IV, p. 123).

(47)   Wood-carving in the Trobriands (*Ill. Arch.*
               p. 107).

(48)   A batch of Irish folklore (*Folk Lore*, IV, p. 349).

(49)   Secular and ceremonial dances of Torres
               Straits (*Internat. Arch. Ethnogr.* VI, p. 131).

(50)   The Aran Islands, Co. Galway: a study in Irish
               ethnography (*Irish Naturalist*, II, p. 303).

(51)   1894.   The decorative art of British New Guinea
               (*R. I. A. Cunningham Memoirs*, X, Dublin).

(52)   Contributions to the anatomy of fishes (with
               T. W. Bridge) (*Proc. Roy. Soc.* LVIII,
               p. 439).

(53)   On the geology of Torres Straits (with W. J.
               Sollas and G. Cole) (*Trans. R.I.A.* XXX,
               p. 419).

(54)   Studies in Irish craniology. Part II. Inishbofin,
               Co. Galway (*Proc. R.I.A.* (3), III, p. 311).

(55)   Ethnography of British New Guinea (*Science
               Progress*, II, p. 83).

(56)   Legends from the Woodlarks, British New
              Guinea (*Folk Lore*, v, p. 316).
(57)   1895. *Evolution in Art*. London.
(58)   Ethnographical studies in the West of Ireland
              (*J. Anthrop. Inst.* xxiv, p. 105).
(59)   Results of 'Challenger' Expedition. VI. An-
              thropology (NATURAL SCIENCE).
(60)   Branched worm-tubes and *Acrozoanthus* (*Proc.
              Roy. Dublin Soc.* N.S. viii, p. 344).
(61)   1896. Peasant life and industries in Ireland (*J. Soc.
              Arts*, xliv, p. 387).
(62)   Neolithic settlement at Whitepark Bay,
              Co. Antrim (*Proc. Camb. Ant. Soc.* ix,
              p. 391).
(63)   On some Actiniaria from Australia (with J. E.
              Duerden) (*Sci. Trans. Roy. Dublin Soc.* (ii),
              vi, p. 139).
(64)   1897. A study of the languages of Torres Straits.
              Part II (with S. H. Ray) (*Proc. R.I.A.* (3),
              iv, p. 119).
(65)   The saving of vanishing knowledge (*Nature*,
              lv, p. 305).
(66)   A plea for a bureau of ethnology for the
              British Empire (*Nature*, lvi, p. 574).
(67)   1898. *The Study of Man* (Progressive Science
              Series), London.
(68)   Studies in Irish craniology. Part III (*Proc.
              R.I.A.* (3), iv, p. 570).
(69)   The Actiniaria of Torres Straits (*Sci. Trans.
              Roy. Dublin Soc.* (2), vi, p. 393).
(70)   Why we measure people (*Science Progress*,
              vii, p. 1).
(71)   *Phellia Sollasi* (*Proc. Roy. Dublin Soc.* N.S.
              viii, p. 693).

(72) 1898. The Cambridge expedition to Torres Straits (*Nature*, LVIII, p. 276).

(73) 1899. The Cambridge expedition to Torres Straits and Sarawak (*Nature*, LX, p. 413).

(74) 1900. A classification of the stone clubs of British New Guinea (*J. Anthrop. Inst.* XXX, p. 221).

(75) Studies in the anthropogeography of British New Guinea (*Geogr. J.* XVI, p. 265).

(76) The evolution of simple societies (*Knowledge*, XVIII).

(77) Decorative art of the Sea Dayaks of Sarawak (*Nature*, LXII, p. 68).

(78) On the textile patterns of the Sea Dayaks (*J. Anthrop. Inst.* XXX, p. 71).

(79) Relics of the stone age in Borneo (*Nature*, LXII, p. 637).

(80) House and family life in Sarawak (*J. Anthrop. Inst.* XXX, p. 71).

(81) A plea for the study of the native races of South Africa (*Nature*, LXIII, p. 187).

(82) 1901. *Head-Hunters, Black, White and Brown.* London.

(83) *Reports of the Cambridge Anthropological Expedition to Torres Straits*, vol. II, i, Cambridge.

(84) On the origin of the Maori scroll design (*Man*, I, p. 68).

(85) A Papuan bow-and-arrow fleam (*Man*, I, p. 145).

(86) The omen animals of Sarawak (*Pop. Sci. Monthly*, LX, p. 80).

(87) Obituary notice of the Rev. J. Chalmers, 'Tamate' (*Nature*, LXIV, p. 39).

(88) 1902. Totemism: Presidential address to Section H
              (*Rep. Brit. Ass.* p. 738).
(89)   What the United States is doing for anthro-
              pology. Presidential address (*J. Anthrop.
              Inst.* xxxii, p. 8).
(90)   A method of recording string figures (with
              W. H. R. Rivers) (*Man*, ii, p. 147).
(91)   Fire-walking in Southern India (*Folk Lore*,
              xiii, p. 89).
(92)   Handbook to the vivaria and fresh-water aqua-
              ria (*Horniman Mus. Handbooks*, L.C.C.).
(93) 1903. *Reports of the Cambridge Anthropological Ex-
              pedition to Torres Straits*, vol. ii, ii, ed.
              A.C.H., Cambridge.
(94)   Anthropology: its position and needs. Presi-
              dential Address (*J. Anthrop. Inst.* xxxiii,
              p. 11).
(95)   The teaching of ethnology at Cambridge: lec-
              tures to missionaries (*Manchester Guardian*,
              Jan. 15).
(96)   The saving of vanishing data (*Pop. Sci.
              Monthly*, lxii, p. 222).
(97)   A few American string figures (*Amer.
              Anthrop.* v, p. 213).
(98)   Folk-lore: the past in the present (*Nat. Home
              Reading Union Mag.*)
(99) 1904. *Reports of the Cambridge Anthropological Ex-
              pedition to Torres Straits*, vol. v, ed.
              A.C.H., Cambridge.
(100)   Drawings by natives of British New Guinea
              (*Man*, iv, p. 33).
(101)   The popularisation of ethnological museums
              (*Nature*, lxx, p. 7).
(102)   Anthropological notes (*Nature*, lxx, p. 138).

(103) 1904. The needs of anthropology at Cambridge (*Nature*, LXX, p. 366).

(104) Handbook to the collection (*Horniman Museum Guide*, L.C.C.).

(105) 1905. Introduction to C. F. Jayne's *String Figures*.

(106) South African ethnology (*Nature*, LXXII, p. 471).

(107) Studies in Bornean decorative art (*Man*, V, p. 67).

(108) Tatuing at Hula, British New Guinea (*Man*, V, p. 86).

(109) Prehistoric cemetery at Harlyn Bay (*Roy. Cornwall Gazette*).

(110) Presidential address to the Cambridge Antiquarian Soc. (*Proc. Camb. Ant. Soc.* XI, p. 285).

(111) 1906. *Magic and Fetishism*. London.

(112) Anthropology at the Universities (with others) (*Man*, VI, p. 85).

(113) A plea for an expedition to Melanesia (*Nature*, LXXIV, p. 187).

(114) The Congress of Americanists at Quebec (*Nature*, LXXIV, p. 595).

(115) String figures from South Africa (*J. Anthrop. Inst.* XXXVI, p. 142).

(116) 1907. *Reports of the Cambridge Anthropological Expedition to Torres Straits*, vol. III, ed. A.C.H., Cambridge.

(117) The religion of the Torres Straits islanders (in *Essays presented to E. B. Tylor*, p. 175).

(118) Burial of amputated limbs (*Folk Lore*, XVIII, p. 216).

(119) 1908. *Reports of the Cambridge Anthropological Expedition to Torres Straits*, vol. VI, ed. A.C.H., Cambridge.

(120)   Art, primitive and savage (in Hastings's *Encyclopaedia of Religion and Ethics*).

(121)   Regulations for obtaining a Diploma of Anthropology in the University of Cambridge (*Man*, VIII, p. 42).

(122)   Copper rod currency from the Transvaal (*Man*, VIII, pp. 121, 183).

(123)   An investigation of the sociology and religion of the Veddas (*Nature*, LXXVIII, p. 201).

(124)   Notes on children's games in British New Guinea (*J. Anthrop. Inst.* XXXVIII, p. 289).

(125)   The Percy Sladen Trust expedition to Melanesia (*Nature*, LXXVIII, p. 393).

(126) 1909. *The Races of Man and their Distribution* London.

(127)   An investigation of the sociology and religion of the Andamanese (*Nature*, LXXIX, p. 345).

(128)   William Ramsay McNab (*Dict. Nat. Biog.*)

(129)   An Imperial Bureau of Anthropology (*Nature*, LXXX, p. 73).

(130)   Copper rod currency of the Balemba (*Folk Lore*, XX, p. 93).

(131)   An anthropological survey of the Sudan (*Nature*, LXXXI, p. 491).

(132) 1910. *History of Anthropology* (with A. H. Quiggin), London.

(133)   New Guinea pygmies (*Nature*, LXXXIII, p. 433).

(134)   Captain Cook Memorial (*Nature*, LXXXV, p. 236).

(135) 1911. *The Wanderings of Peoples*. Cambridge.

(136)   Dr Frazer on totemism and exogamy (*Soc. Rev.* IV, p. 37).

(137) 1911. Human Societies: a lecture to U.C.W. Sci.
               Soc. Aberystwyth (*The Dragon*, XXXIII,
               p. 223).

(138)   The Cambridge Anthropological Expedition to
               Western Australia (*Nature*, LXXXVII, p. 24).

(139)   The First Universal Races Congress (*Science*,
               N.S. XXXIV, p. 304).

(140) 1912. The anthropological survey of Canada (*Nature*,
               LXXXVIII, p. 597).

(141)   Ethics among primitive people (*Expository
               Times*, XXIII, p. 403).

(142)   The 18th International Congress of Ameri-
               canists (*Nature*, LXXXIX, p. 357).

(143)   *Reports of the Cambridge Anthropological Ex-
               pedition to Torres Straits*, vol. IV, Cambridge.

(144)   The houses of New Guinea (in *Festskrift
               tillägnad Eduard Westermarck*), Helsinki.

(145)   The Pygmy question (Appendix to A. F. R.
               Wollaston's *Pygmies and Papuans*).

(146)   The physical characters of the races and
               peoples of Borneo (Appendix to C. Hose
               and W. McDougall's *Pagan Tribes of
               Borneo*).

(147) 1913. An ascent of the Snow Mountains of New
               Guinea (*Science*, N.S. XXXVIII, p. 44).

(148)   The outrigger canoes of Torres Straits and
               North Queensland (in *Essays presented to
               [Sir] W. Ridgeway*).

(149)   Heroes and hero-gods (in Hastings's *Encyclo-
               paedia of Religion and Ethics*).

(150) 1914. The soul of the red man (*R.P.A. Annual*,
               p. 39).

(151) 1915. Introduction to Sarat Chandra Roy's *Orans of
               Chota Nagpur*

(152)   1916.   Kava-drinking in New Guinea (*Man*, XVI, p. 145).

(153)   The Kabiri or Girara district, Fly River (*J. Roy. Anthrop. Inst.* XLVI, p. 334).

(154)   Obituary notices of Sir Laurence Gomme (*Man*, XVI, p. 86: *Nature*, XCVII, p. 11).

(155)   1917.   Five new religious cults in British New Guinea (with E. W. P. Chinnery) (*Hibbert J.* XV, p. 448).

(156)   Negrillos and Negritos (in Hastings's *Encyclopaedia of R. & E.*).

(157)   New Guinea (in Hastings's *Encyclopaedia of R. & E.*).

(158)   Obituary notice of Sir E. B. Tylor (*Nature*, XCVIII, p. 373).

(159)   Three days in the thick of it (*Red Triangle*, III, p. 652).

(160)   Note on the Gogodara (Kabiri or Girara) (*Man*, XVII, p. 193).

(161)   1918.   The outrigger canoe of East Africa (*Man*, XVIII, p. 49).

(162)   The influence of natural conditions on simple human societies (*Geogr. Teacher*, IX, p. 244).

(163)   Melanesian influence in Easter Island (*Folk Lore*, XXIX, p. 161).

(164)   An anomalous form of outrigger attachment in Torres Straits (*Man*, XVIII, p. 113).

(165)   The Agiba cult of the Kerewa culture (*Man*, XVIII, p. 177).

(166)   1919.   *The Wanderings of Peoples*, 2nd ed. Cambridge.

(167)   Presidential address to the Folk-Lore Society (*Folk Lore*, XXX).

(168)   The Kopiravi cult of the Namau, Papua (*Man*, XIX, p. 177).

(169) 1920. The outriggers of Indonesian canoes (*J. Roy. Anthrop. Inst.* L, p. 69).

(170) Migrations of culture in British New Guinea (Huxley Memorial lecture) (*J. Roy. Anthrop. Inst.* L, p. 237).

(171) *Man, Past and Present*, revised edition (with A. H. Quiggin), Cambridge.

(172) 1921. *The Practical Value of Ethnology* (Conway Memorial lecture), London.

(173) Racial and cultural distributions in New Guinea (*Geogr. Teacher*, XII, p. 15).

(174) 1922. Obituary notices of W. H. R. Rivers (*Man*, XXII, p. 97; *Nature*, CIX, p. 786).

(175) 1923. Stuffed heads from New Guinea (*Man*, XXIII, p. 4).

(176) *A Brief History of the Study of Anthropology at Cambridge.*

(177) A new form of mask from the Sepik, Papua (*Man*, XXIII, p. 81).

(178) Migrations of peoples in the south-west Pacific (*Proc. Pan-Pacific Sci. Congress*, Australia, I, p. 220).

(179) 1924. *The Races of Man and their Distribution*, revised edition, Cambridge.

(180) Anthropology at the 2nd Pan-Pacific Science Congress, Australia (*Man*, XXIV, p. 12).

(181) The peopling of the Pacific (*Discovery*, V, p. 11).

(182) The cultural history of the Pacific (*Discovery*, V, p. 40).

(183) The 'White Indians' of Panama (with others) (*Man*, XXIV, p. 162).

(184) 1925. Pearls as 'givers of life' (*Man*, XXIV, p. 177; XXV, p. 51).

(185) 1926. Obituary notices of Sir W. Ridgeway (*Nature*, cxviii, p. 275; *Man*, xxvi, p. 175).

(186) 1927. Introduction to G. Landtman's *Kiwai Papuans of British New Guinea*.

(187) 1928. Introduction to W. E. Armstrong's *Rossel Island*.

(188) The cult of Waiet in Torres Straits (*Mem. Queensland Mus.* ix, ii, p. 406).

(189) Environment and cultural progress among primitive peoples (Herbertson memorial lecture) (*Geogr.* xiv, p. 406).

(190) Social constructiveness (*Brit. J. Psychol.* xviii, p. 400).

(191) Racial zones and head indices (*Nature*, cxxii, p. 96).

(192) Obituary notices of Baron A. von Hügel (*Man*, xxviii, p. 169; *Nature*, cxxii, p. 322).

(193) 1929. *The Religion of a Primitive People* (Frazer lecture).

(194) Obituary notice of Charles Hose (*Nature*, cxxiv, p. 845).

(195) Obituary notices of Edward Clodd (*Folk Lore*, xl, p. 183; *Nature*, cxxv, p. 536).

(196) 1930. Introduction to [Sir] E. B. Tylor's *Anthropology*.

(197) Smoking in Papua (*Nature*, cxxvi, p. 255).

(198) A new method of smoking tobacco in Papua (*Man*, xxx, p. 133).

(199) 1931. Tobacco in New Guinea (*Amer. Anthrop.* xxxiii, p. 657).

(200) Notes on carved *gopi* boards from the Papuan Gulf (with H. Braunholtz) (*Man*, xxxi, p. 58).

(201) The antiquity of Man in Tanganyika Territory (*Camb. Rev.* lii, p. 46).

(202)   1932.   A prehistoric sherd from the Mailu district,
Papua (*Man*, XXXII, p. 111).

(203)   1933.   A stone bowl from New Britain (with V. H.
Sherwin) (*Man*, XXXIII, p. 160).

(204)   Preface to A. B. Deacon's *Malekula*.

(205)   1934.   Appreciation (in *Essays presented to C. G.
Seligman*).

(206)   Obituary notices of J. H. Holmes (*Man*, XXXIV,
p. 92; *Nature*, CXXXIII, p. 861).

(207)   Sectional Proceedings of the International
Congress of Anthropological and Ethno-
logical Sciences (*Man*, XXXIV, p. 146).

(208)   1935.   *Reports of the Cambridge Anthropological Expedition to Torres Straits*, vol. I, Cambridge.

(209)   *We Europeans* (with J. Huxley and A. M.
Carr-Saunders), London.

(210)   The racial question in theory and fact (with
J. Huxley) (*Antiquity*, IX, p. 261).

(211)   Racial myths and ethnic fallacies (with J.
Huxley) (*Discovery*, XVI, p. 252).

(212)   1936.   *Iban or Sea Dayak Fabrics* (with L. E. Start),
Cambridge.

(213)   Introduction to Lord Moyne's *Walkabout*.

(214)   Introduction to F. E. Williams's *Papuans of
the Trans-Fly*.

(215)   *Canoes of Oceania* (with J. Hornell), Honolulu.

(216)   1937.   Anthropology (in *The March of Science*, p. 73).

(217)   1939.   Obituary notices of S. H. Ray (*Nature*, CXLIII,
p. 149; *Man*, XXXIX, p. 58).

(218)   Obituary notice of Henry Balfour (Obit. of the
Royal Society).

(219)   1940.   Obituary notice of Sir Hubert Murray (*Man*,
XL, p. 89).

(220)   *Smoking and Tobacco Pipes in New Guinea*. (In
the Press.)

INDEX

167

CAMBRIDGE: PRINTED BY W. LEWIS, M.A., AT THE UNIVERSITY PRESS